The
Window at
St. Catherine's

The
Window at
St. Catherine's

John F. Dobbertin, Jr.

iUniverse, Inc.

New York Lincoln Shanghai

The Window at St. Catherine's

iUniverse books may be ordered through booksellers or by contacting:

iUniverse
2021 Pine Lake Road, Suite 100
Lincoln, NE 68512
www.iuniverse.com
1-800-Authors (1-800-288-4677)

ISBN-13: 978-0-595-36921-8 (pbk)
ISBN-13: 978-0-595-81333-9 (ebk)
ISBN-10: 0-595-36921-9 (pbk)
ISBN-10: 0-595-81333-X (ebk)

Printed in the United States of America

To the members of the
355th Fighter Group
8th United States Army Air Force
and
All their English friends

Contents

In a country church 15 miles south of Cambridge, England, there is a large stained glass window made by a *Yank* honoring the 355th Fighter Group of the 8th United States Army Air Force in World War Two. Our story begins with a sport fishing tale and takes us back to the most incredible account of any World War Two American fighter ace. It is also the story of a remarkable friendship spanning four decades. This is the true story of *The Window at St. Catherine's*.

PART I
Meeting Bill Cullerton

1

Do You Fish?

This cold, late April morning begins with the drive to Johnson Motor's Plant Six located smack on Lake Michigan. The spectacular location makes up for the factorylike offices, divided by gray steel knee-walls topped with a kind of opaque, corrugated glass.

There is no question I am at the bottom of the corporate public relations ladder. I have my University of Michigan degree in journalism, followed by a two-year Michigan fellowship as subeditor of *The Daily-Star,* Beirut, Lebanon. At age 25 I know public relations is what I want to be doing. The pay is lousy but the work is interesting...and different, always different. Since my first day on the job in January no two days have been the same.

Working away typing a press release I hear our boss, Public Relations Director John Tuzee exclaim:

"Hang on to your desks boys, Cullerton is here!"

I walk out to meet our visitor.

"Hey, John Tuzee, how are you!" Cullerton said, thrusting his right hand forward to greet Tuzee.

"Great, Bill, just great. And look at you...look at that Florida tan! Man, you've been fishing all winter!" Tuzee said.

"Chasing those marlin," Bill replies.

"You haven't met the others," Tuzee said. "Let me warn you, we have an annual budget and this guy is here to raid the place. And look at the time. It's barely eight o'clock and Bill had to drive up here all the way from Elmhurst. What time did you leave, man!"

This is my introduction to Bill Cullerton, a handsome Irishman from Chicago by my guess in his mid-forties. He is very carefully dressed in a nicely-tailored sport coat, tie, well-pressed slacks and highly-polished shoes.

"Bill here is a fishing tackle manufacturer's rep," Tuzee explains. "He sells only the very best fishing tackle to about five customers—Sears, Wards, Ace Hardware," Tuzee starts to laugh.

"Keep going," Bill said breaking into a broad grin.

"But mostly he goes fishing and gets his picture on the covers of all the outdoor magazines," Tuzee said. "And, of course we like that—especially when he is leaning over a Johnson outboard."

"I do that a lot," Cullerton said.

The deal is Cullerton receives the very latest Johnson outboard motor for a year on what is called *consignment,* then he returns it and picks up a new one. The cost comes out of the Johnson Motors public relations budget—our budget!

"What's this going to cost me this year?" Tuzee said, feigning a frown.

"A couple of those new 25 horsepower Johnson Sea-Horses would look really great on my new Lund boat," Bill said.

"You had one consignment outboard last year. Two this year!" Tuzee said, throwing his arms up in the air in mock horror.

"Hey, it'll be worth it," Bill said. "Besides, I think we're going to be doing some fishing on some larger lakes this year."

There was a very large clue of a major development here that goes right past all of us.

"You drive a tough deal, Cullerton. But they're yours. There goes the budget, boys!" Tuzee said with a shrug.

Tuzee knows from experience that putting Johnson outboards in Bill's hands is as good as putting money in the bank for the Johnson Motors public relations department. Cullerton's picture appears at least once a year on the cover of almost every major outdoor and sport fishing publication in the United States. And those photos do not accidentally include a Johnson outboard. Many are taken by professional photographers hired by Johnson Motors. Composition of the photos is very carefully arranged in a vertical format to ensure they will be suitable for magazine covers. Great four-color negatives are provided—for free, of course—to the outdoor magazines. Much of the photography is done at Cypress Gardens, Florida, under an exclusive deal with Johnson Motors. Johnson outboards also pull those beautiful Cypress Gardens water-ski gals.

His deal done with Tuzee, the good salesman Cullerton is, he moves over and starts a conversation with me. Nevermind I am the lowest man in the public relations department, or for that matter the lowest person in the entire Johnson Motors marketing area.

"So tell me, do you like to fish?" Bill asks.

"Absolutely, yes," I reply. "I grew up on a lake in Michigan. Had my own boat and fished from the time I can remember."

Well, that is all it takes. Bill wants my card and he gives me his. Bill has found someone in the Johnson Motors public relations department who knows something about fishing. From that moment I am *Bill's guy* at Johnson Motors.

Turning to leave, Cullerton raises his hand in the air, index finger extended and says to me: "I'll be in touch."

◆   ◆   ◆

It is wonderful living next to an inland sea over 100 miles wide and 300 miles long and up to 900 feet deep. It is also a little weird to realize there isn't a fish out there more than a foot long. Millions of sport fishermen live within easy driving distance of this vast body of water. To them Lake Michigan is a wasteland, an enormous freshwater dead sea.

The Johnson Motors parking lot is directly in front of our offices, facing the water.

Climbing from the car I am immediately welcomed this clear May morning by the most gut-wrenching stench of rotting fish. I had walked on the sidewalks of Beirut in 100-degree weather during a two-month strike by the refuse collectors with garbage stacked higher than cars and it hadn't smelled this bad.

There is an unusual wind blowing across the cold water from the east. Normally the prevailing winds are from the west, blowing out across the lake. And the wind from the east reeks of putrid fish.

"You look like you're smelling something you don't like," our receptionist said as she walks toward the office building.

"What is it?" I ask.

"Oh, that's right, you're new here. That is the lovely scent of rotting alewives. Get used to it. It's our spring and early summer perfume," she said. "When the wind is from the east, the newly deceased little devils wash up on the beach."

I stop for a moment and watch the trawler *Mathon* chug out of Waukegan harbor. At least they were optimistic there might be some perch in Lake Michigan worth trying to catch.

As I enter the office the telephone is ringing.

"Bill Cullerton for you," the receptionist said.

"Hello, Bill," I said.

"How's John this morning?" Bill asks.

"Pretty good except for the horrible stench blowing in off Lake Michigan as I came in from the parking lot," I said.

"I think the fisheries boys over in Michigan have figured out a way to take care of that problem," Bill said. "They've planted hundreds-of-thousands of salmon that will eat those alewives. And you're probably not going to believe this, but there are salmon swimming in Lake Michigan not more than a quarter-mile from where you're sitting."

"Bill, you're right. That is going to take a leap of faith here. The only thing out in that lake are those stinking alewives and maybe some perch, if Mathon hasn't caught them all. His trawler was headed out this morning," I said.

"Good for Mathon. But I'm telling you, those salmon are out there. Can you arrange a boat to take us out tomorrow to see if we can catch a few?" Bill asks.

"I think you're nuts, but I'll have the boat ready to go," I said.

"If you have the boat, I'll bring the fishing tackle. We're going to catch some salmon tomorrow," Bill said. "I'll be there by 8:30."

"Meet me at my office. We'll go from the test docks back by the engineering department," I said.

◆   ◆   ◆

The Johnson Motors engineers are running tests on the brand new Johnson "191," a 19-foot tri-hull with a 122-horsepower inboard-outboard drive. It rides high out of the water, with three-feet of freeboard making it a good boat for fishing within a half-mile-or-so of the Lake Michigan shoreline. There is a "191" at the test docks located right on Waukegan harbor, and that will be our fishing rig for the day.

Bill Cullerton and I make our way through the Johnson Motors plant into the engineering department where we are instantly a curiosity. In the first place, we are in their way. In white shirts and ties, slide rules attached to their belts, the engineers mix with craftsmen in their coveralls as they design and handcraft parts for prototype engines. These guys are on a serious mission to build better outboard motors.

You can read what is going through their well-organized, disciplined minds: What are these public relations types doing carting a mountain of fishing tackle back to the test docks? If they want to go fishing, why don't they just go back to Florida. Hell, those PR guys all have tans year-around—just look at them!

We carefully load the boat with Bill Cullerton's Johnson rods and reels, Plano tackle boxes, Rapala fishing lures, and a cooler. We have enough fishing gear in the boat to outfit a half-dozen fishermen.

This is lesson-number-one when fishing with Bill Cullerton: Always use the best equipment and be sure you bring plenty of it. And, of course, you fish with all the brands Bill sells to major distributors and the huge retailers of the day.

As we clear the breakwater at Waukegan harbor, we see very gentle swells on the surface of Lake Michigan. There is a very light southerly breeze. Although the water temperature is still cool—maybe 50 degrees—the bright morning sun warms us.

"OK, set a gentle trolling speed and we'll put a couple of lines out about 100 or 150 feet-or-so with Raps," Bill said.

Bill starts pulling rods and reels out of their wrappings and sets about attaching the lures to the lines.

"Two good friends of mine at Normark Corporation up in the Twin Cities were over in Finland and fell in love with these handmade, balsawood lures. They bought 5,000 of them at a buck-a-piece from the manufacturer," Bill said. "That means they've got to retail for almost twice that. I told them they were crazy. The world had moved to plastic lures costing the average fisherman about a buck. Heck, I wasn't even interested in taking them on. But then I fished with Raps up in Lake of The Woods and boy did we catch big fish with these lures. Raps swim in a straight line and appear to predators to be separated from other small fish so the big fish think they're easy pickings," Bill said. "And what do these Raps look like?"

I take a quick look over my shoulder as Bill holds a Rapala lure up in the air.

"A lot like the stinking alewives," I said.

"I think our salmon are going to love these Raps," Bill said.

"Fill me in on the salmon you think are out here," I said with more than a hint of doubt in my voice.

"That stench you smelled yesterday morning from those dead and dying alewives gave the Michigan Fisheries guys the idea they could make lemonade out of lemons," Bill said.

Bill pauses as he casts the Rapala out over the transom.

"First of all, you know they've controlled the sea lamprey-eels that came in from the St. Lawrence and destroyed almost every decent size fish in the Great Lakes," Bill said. "Now we've got millions of these small alewives that have no predators. So they're dying by the millions and stinking up our shorelines. No one thinks alewives are good for anything except maybe cat food. But think about it. Big fish eat little fish. What we need are some big fish. And while we're at it, how about some great game fish for Midwest sportsmen."

"And what could be better than salmon," I said.

"That's the exact conclusion the Michigan Fisheries guys came to, and that's what they planted two years ago. Both coho and chinook," Bill said.

"Where?" I ask.

"In several streams in Michigan. They concentrated on rivers around Manistee for starters," Bill said. "They got the salmon eggs from Oregon and Washington, and away they went. They planted hundreds of thousands of salmon. If it works out, they'll be planting millions every year."

"And now you're telling me we've got the State of Michigan's salmon over here by Waukegan, Illinois?" I ask.

"The salmon are released as fingerlings into the Michigan rivers. Each river has its own scent and the salmon remember the scent of the river in which they're released. Then they take off and move around in the big water of the Great Lakes. The Michigan Fisheries guys have been tracking them. The salmon are following concentrations of alewives, and they're moving with the major, natural currents in Lake Michigan," Bill said, playing out the second line. "And that takes them right past Waukegan."

This is the first large clue Bill is working with inside knowledge. Bill carefully calculated this fishing trip as to time and place. I am learning. Bill Cullerton does not go on wild goose chases. Things are done with purpose.

"So what happens with these salmon as they get bigger?" I ask.

"As with all salmon as they mature, they'll swim back to their point of birth—back to the beds in the rivers where they were released. They follow those distinctive scents to their home stream to reproduce and then die," Bill said. "Right now, we're fishing for what we call *jack salmon*—or immature salmon. These fish will grow—I'm guessing—to be in the six to ten pound class for coho and much bigger for the chinook."

As I pilot the boat and think about what Bill is saying, I am looking around for any other boat traffic. The view is nothing but empty water for miles to the east, north and south. We are absolutely the only boat out as we head north, about a quarter-mile away from the entrance to Waukegan harbor. We are directly in front of the Johnson Motors factories with 3,000 employees who are all hard at work building outboard motors and the newer inboard-outboards like the one we are using this day.

"How are we for trolling speed?" I ask.

"Cut her back just a bit," Bill said. "Action on the Raps might be a bit too fast."

"So if we catch salmon today, how big will they be?" I ask.

"I'm going to let you in on a little secret here," Bill said, lifting one of the rods to check the action on the Rap. "The Michigan fisheries guys have been working with their pals over in Illinois and they've been netting coho salmon of two-to-three pounds not very far from right here."

And at that, one of the reels starts a high-pitched whining sound as line peels off. Bill grabs the rod and raises the tip to set the lure.

"*That* is not a perch," Bill said, as he lets the reel continue spinning line off.

"Here, take this other rod and reel in the line so we're not knitting sweaters out there," Bill said.

I slip the boat into neutral, grab the rod and begin quickly reeling in the second line.

Suddenly about 200 feet off port a fish jumps three feet out of the water.

"Look at that!" Bill exclaims. "That's our salmon!"

Bill begins carefully reeling in line. Then he lets more line peel off as the salmon makes another run.

"Man this is great fun!" Bill exclaims.

Watching Bill you might think this is the first and maybe biggest fish he has ever caught. I know better because after we first met I read a press release on Bill. I am now fishing with the youngest member ever elected to the Sport Fishing Hall of Fame. Bill holds several world records for fish he caught—both freshwater and saltwater. Bill never outgrows the thrill of the tussle with a fish on the line.

"Hey, John, grab the net," Bill said, nodding toward the net braced against the seat.

Bill continues letting the fish take some line and then carefully raising the rod tip and reeling, working the fish toward the boat.

"We're going to take our time here and make sure this guy is a little tired before we try the net," Bill said, watching the fish peel off some more line. "This is one fish we want in the cooler."

Net in hand I move toward the transom.

"OK, now we've got to keep this guy from going under the boat or wrapping the line around the prop," Bill said. He again raises the rod tip and then swings it toward the bow.

There—right there next to the boat—is the first flash of a nice-sized fish.

"Get that net behind him when I swing the rod forward," Bill said.

I dip the net deep in the water, letting the net flow. I bring the net up behind the fish and in one motion sweep it right up under the fish and swing it into the boat.

"Would you look at that," Bill said reaching in the net and carefully picking the fish up by the gills. "John, this is a coho salmon."

We have our silver, two-pound salmon in the boat. It is a beautiful fish—bluish-green along the dorsal fin, striking silver on the flanks and bright white in the belly area.

There were few sport fishermen in the entire country who would believe we actually caught a salmon off Waukegan. It is stunning.

When I was growing up in Michigan we caught a lot of bluegills, sunfish, largemouth bass and the occasional small pike on inland lakes. Here is a salmon. Salmon are a special fish you catch in Scotland where you hire a *gillie* for your guide to fish on the private and protected salmon rivers, or you go out in the Pacific Ocean off the coast of Washington or Oregon in deep-sea sport fishing rigs. Nobody catches salmon in the Midwest in Lake Michigan.

"Into the cooler," Bill said. He removes the Rapala's hooks from the salmon's jaw.

"Now, let's go for another one," Bill said.

And here I learn another lesson about the driving force that is Bill Cullerton. You've nailed one coho salmon, a fish almost no one would believe could be found anywhere in this lake. One coho in the cooler would be good enough for most folks to prove the salmon are out here. Not Bill.

Let's go for another one. Let's prove this is not a fluke. We're good. Let's go catch more coho.

Bill casts out the first line. That's when I notice he is left-handed. I look at his hands. They are small, almost delicate. When he places the lure on the fishing line it is done very gracefully, carefully. The second line goes out and we resume a very slow troll.

We are warmed by the sun as the engine hums and the boat gently rocks through the small swells. A chilling breeze picks up for a moment rippling along the cold Lake Michigan surface and we again abandon all thought of taking off our light jackets.

"You know, I've been thinking," Bill said. "Nobody is going to believe we actually caught this salmon on Lake Michigan!"

"Well, Bill, it is a stretch," I said. "I'm not certain I would believe it if I hadn't been here to see it."

I am still processing what I have seen. In my lifetime I was certain no one had caught a salmon in the southern end of Lake Michigan—maybe not in the Great Lakes, period. In fact, not many fishermen had caught anything in Lake Michigan bigger than a 12-inch perch. Even the bigger perch would sometimes have lamprey-eel marks on their flanks. Real sport fishermen didn't bother wetting their lines in Lake Michigan.

We continue moving slowly along the Waukegan waterfront, not more than a quarter-mile offshore. We run about a mile to the north and then swing around back to the south. We are still the only boat in sight. The gentle rocking motion and a light sound of the water slapping at the boat is almost a lullaby, extremely relaxing.

"Hey, there it goes!" Bill exclaims.

Once again there is the high-pitched sound of line peeling off the reel.

I put the boat in neutral, grab the second line and reel it in.

Within a few minutes the second coho salmon is in the cooler.

"I think we should go in and have some lunch and make a couple of telephone calls," Bill said.

"How about Mathon's?" I suggest.

"Where else!" Bill said.

Mathon's Restaurant is a 1960s Chicago area landmark. It is just a stone's throw from Waukegan harbor, and almost as close to the Johnson Motors factories. Owner, impresario, restaurateur Mathon Kyritsis is known throughout Greater Chicago. His ancient trawler—*Mathon*—regularly scours the southern end of Lake Michigan for perch. Every year Mathon makes all the Chicago area newspapers, radio stations and television stations with his weather predictions based on how deep or shallow the perch were in Lake Michigan. His amusing presentation of his perch-weather-forecast always provides a lighter moment for all of northern Illinois. And it is pretty good for Mathon's Restaurant business as well. Of course, Lake Michigan perch is the specialty of the house.

After unloading the boat and carefully placing the cooler with its precious cargo in the back of Bill's station wagon, we enter Mathon's Restaurant. Bill strides directly to the pay telephone, whips out his pocket directory, deposits several quarters and dials.

"Hey, Tom. It's Bill Cullerton."

It is quiet enough I can hear the voice of the person Bill called.

"What the heck are you up to today?" the person asks.

"I'm calling you from Mathon's Restaurant. We've been out on the Lake and I have two coho salmon in the cooler," Bill said.

"You're full of Irish bullshit," is the response from the other end of the line.

"Why don't you come up here tomorrow…." Bill puts his hand over the telephone and looks at me and said: "I've got Tom McNally on the line here. Can you have the boat ready to go tomorrow?"

"You bet," I said.

Any Midwest sportsman knows Tom McNally is the outdoor editor of the *Chicago Tribune*. His Sunday column—*Woods & Waters*—is *the* outdoor column in the entire Midwest. The Sunday *Chicago Tribune* is over a one-million circulation newspaper, one of the biggest in the United States.

"Tom, we'll see you in Waukegan tomorrow at 8:30," Bill said.

◆   ◆   ◆

The next day Bill Cullerton quickly introduces Tom McNally and we are on our way through the Johnson Motors plant to the test docks.

The hard-working, intense, engineers in their white shirts and ties are less than impressed when the three of us appear loaded with more fishing tackle to board the Johnson "191." This makes two days in a row of these tanned public relations types disrupting their serious work. What in hell is going on?

We clear the breakwater at the entrance to Waukegan harbor and enter Lake Michigan.

"Cullerton, if you've brought me up here on a lark I am going to be pissed," McNally almost growls.

McNally is a tall fellow whose head seems to tilt forward. He is wearing wire-rimed glasses and a baseball-style cap. There is something about the teeth. They are often bared in an almost Teddy Roosevelt look, teeth clamped together, lips pulled back. It isn't quite a grin and it isn't a grimace—it is something in-between. In the brief moments we have been together, I have not been able to size up this extremely important person. When McNally writes in his *Woods & Waters* column that it is time to clean out the mess in your tackle box, by golly thousands of tackle boxes are pulled from garages and basements throughout the Greater Chicago area and they are cleaned. When McNally writes they were catching bass in the Chain of Lakes on minnows, there is a run on bait shops and the minnows are gone. If it is in Tom McNally's Sunday *Woods & Waters* column, it is *God's Truth* about the outdoor sporting scene that week.

"We caught two out here yesterday. Now let's see if we can do better," Bill said. "Hey, John, wherever you took us yesterday let's do it again today."

"You've got it, Bill," I said as we take a heading due north, about a quarter-mile off the shoreline.

Lake Michigan is almost flat, just a ripple here and there when a light breeze brushes the water. Bright sunshine warms us as we slowly churn north.

"So you used Raps?" McNally asks.

"Worked like a charm. Just put them out there about 150 feet and we troll fairly slow," Bill said.

"OK, give me one of those Raps," McNally said.

The more I hear McNally's almost gruff voice, the more I begin to think of him as not a warm and fuzzy fellow.

"Hey, John, speed us up just a notch," Bill said.

"Right, just a notch," I reply, easing the boat to a slightly greater speed.

"And you might try slow zigzags," Bill said.

I begin easing the boat to deeper water, then back toward shore in very slow arcs. We turn back, heading south and keeping up the slow turns. On this Wednesday morning we have the entire shoreline off Waukegan for the miles we can see over the open water all to ourselves. There is not another boat in sight.

"Holy shit!" McNally exclaims as I hear the now familiar high-pitched whining of line off the reel.

Cullerton rapidly reels in his line to clear the water for McNally.

"Easy there, Tom," Bill said in a very calm tone.

"Look at that!" McNally holds the rod with one hand and points about 150 feet to starboard as his hooked salmon springs three feet in the air. "For holy crying out loud, would you just look at that!" McNally exclaims, shaking his head in total disbelief and grabbing his fishing rod with both hands. "Who the hell would believe we've got salmon off Waukegan."

We return to shore for another lunch at Mathon's Restaurant. This time we have three coho salmon in the cooler.

◆　　　◆　　　◆

Sunday morning I open the *Chicago Tribune,* rip out the sports section and immediately turn to Tom McNally's *Woods & Waters* column. And there is the story about our Wednesday fishing outing. Tom McNally announces to the world that salmon are to be caught in Lake Michigan right off Waukegan, Illinois. The bait to use: Rapalas—preferably the bluish ones that look the most like alewives. There is no mention of Johnson Motors or the Johnson "191" boat we used that day. So far I am batting zero for my employer.

◆   ◆   ◆

The following Saturday morning I drove down to Waukegan harbor.

Empty boat trailers jam the lakefront parking area. More trucks and cars with empty boat trailers attached are parked at crazy angles all over the nearby streets. There are four-block long lines of vehicles pulling boat trailers waiting their turn at the boat-launch ramp. Looking out over the water just outside the harbor entrance it appears as if you could walk across Lake Michigan on the decks of the huge fleet of sport fishing boats. They are out there bow-to-stern, gunwale-to-gunwale. Fishing poles fill the horizon almost as dense as cornstalks in an Illinois farm field in late August.

They had read Tom McNally's *Woods & Waters* column the preceding Sunday. If McNally said there were salmon in Lake Michigan just off Waukegan, then as certain as God created the sun and the moon there would be salmon to be caught. They believed the *Gospel According to McNally* and they are all out there, after those coho.

◆   ◆   ◆

Bill Cullerton is my first call this Monday morning.

"How's John this morning?" Bill asks.

"Man, Bill have you heard what happened in Waukegan over the weekend?" I ask.

"A few fishermen out there, were there?" Bill laughs. "Yah, I heard all about it. Crazy, isn't it?"

"I think we started something," I said.

"Our telephones won't stop ringing here," Bill said. "I've got every distributor and bait shop owner from Dubuque to Peoria trying to order

Raps. Hell, nobody's got any for 500 miles around Waukegan. We're calling Normark up in the Twin Cities and they're calling Finland. I'll tell you, the lights will be burning late tonight at the Rapala factory in Finland! But that's not why I'm calling. I had a call this morning from Jack Griffin at the *Sun-Times.*"

Jack Griffin is probably the finest sports columnist writing at the time for a Chicago newspaper. His tightly-written columns on all sports from boxing to baseball to fishing flow in the most graceful way, always leaving you with a special message.

"Well Grif had a call from his boss and he wants to catch some salmon in Lake Michigan," Bill said.

"You mean the sports editor of the *Chicago Sun-Times?*" I ask.

"Not quite," Bill said. "It's the publisher, the owner—Marshall Field. Do you think you could arrange the boat for tomorrow?"

"No problem," I said.

◆　　　◆　　　◆

If there is a name more Chicagoan than Marshall Field, I have no idea who it could be.

Everyone in the United States—and for that matter most of the civilized world—knows about the Marshall Field's Store on State Street in Chicago's Loop. Nine stories tall and occupying a city block, Marshall Field's is the Midwest's premier emporium. Marshall Field's is to Chicago what Macy's is to New York and what Harrod's is to London. Every woman shopper who lives in Chicago and every woman shopper who comes to Chicago makes a beeline for Marshall Field's the moment they arrive in *The Loop.* Directly south and across the street from the main store at this time is Marshall Field's Men's Store—a true gentleman's store—complete with the world's finest fishing and hunting gear.

The Marshall Field empire stretches way beyond the retail store. It includes two of Chicago's leading newspapers of the day, the morning *Chicago Sun-Times* and the evening *Chicago Daily-News.*

From the time this empire was founded in 1865 by the original Marshall Field, there have been several generations all with the same family name. I begin asking around to find out which Marshall Field this one might be. No one seems quite certain. Guesses are he would be either Marshall Field III...or maybe IV...or possibly V. It really is of no consequence. No one refers to this gentleman by his Roman numerals. He is very simply *the* Marshall Field. And he is coming to Waukegan to board the Johnson "191" boat and go after those salmon that are right here, in his backyard.

◆   ◆   ◆

Pulling up in front of the Johnson Motors plant the next morning I can see whitecaps on Lake Michigan. This is not a good sign.

I get out of the car and cross the road for a better look across the beach. There are swells of at least five feet with a crossing wind creating a swirling whipping cream of whitecaps. Wind is from almost due north and it is cold.

This is not a day for fishing on Lake Michigan. Indeed, there is not a boat to be seen.

I return to the parking lot and a moment later Bill Cullerton arrives with two passengers.

"John, I want you to meet Marshall Field and Jack Griffin," Bill said, as the three walk from Bill's car.

Chicago Sun-Times sports columnist Jack Griffin is about my height, stocky, round-jawed with very intense blue eyes. He looks and talks a little like Humphrey Bogart.

Marshall Field is young—he appears to be in his mid-thirties—slim and rather tall compared to the rest of us.

"Have you seen the lake this morning?" I ask.

"What do you think?" Bill asks.

"Pretty rough. Unfortunately, I think we're skunked," I said.

Bill nods.

"I'll tell you what. We'll save the salmon for another day and we'll go out to McGraw," Marshall Field suggests.

As a newcomer to the area, I have never heard of "McGraw." But if Marshall Field thinks "McGraw" is a good idea, then it's "McGraw."

◆   ◆   ◆

The Max McGraw Wildlife Foundation preserve is located just north of Elgin, Illinois, about 40 miles west of Chicago near the Fox River and the small town of Dundee.

Looking at the calm water on the small lake in this wildlife refuge, you would never guess the surf was up on Lake Michigan.

Cullerton and Marshall Field take one small boat and Jack Griffin and I take the other. We row out and begin casting. Mostly Grif and I watch Cullerton and Marshall Field as we pretend to be interested in our fishing. We are too far away from them to hear any conversation, but they seem to be doing fine.

"How well do you know Cullerton?" Jack Griffin asks.

"We met about two months ago and we've been on a couple of day fishing trips for salmon," I said.

"Did you know that if Butch O'Hare had survived World War Two and Bill Cullerton had died, we would all be flying in and out of Cullerton International?" Grif asks.

"I had no idea," I said.

"Bill was Illinois' leading fighter ace in the war," Grif said. "He destroyed 28 Nazi planes. Quite a record. There were two names considered when the politicians named Chicago's new airport. Butch O'Hare died during the war. So the pols reasoned Cullerton was still alive and he could do something really terrible...like shoot his mother. Butch O'Hare, on the other hand, was dead. So...we fly in and out of O'Hare."

"Does Bill ever talk about his experiences in the war?" I ask.

"Never," Grif said. "He'll just say: 'That was in another life.'"

◆   ◆   ◆

"Have you got a moment?" John Tuzee asks as he walks into my office.
For your boss, there is always time!

"I've been thinking about how we can take advantage of this salmon
boom in the Great Lakes. I think we should take the new Johnson '191,'
strip it down and outfit it as a Great Lakes sport fishing boat. What do you
think?" Tuzee asks.

"Terrific idea," I said.

"Call Cullerton and see if he can help us. Then call the accessories guys
and let them know what we're up to," Tuzee said. "I'll call the boat factory
and tell them to send a powered-up boat with just seats, pilot's wheel and
windscreen—no carpet, nothing else."

Bill Cullerton arrives two days later laden with equipment. Of course
everything he brings, he sells.

We take all the equipment over to the nearby Johnson Motors accessories plant. The boat is already there.

We set about creating the most complete sport fishing boat ever rigged
for Great Lakes sport fishing. We have two fish-locators, ship-to-shore
radio, outriggers for deepwater trolling, dual fighting chairs with rod-hold-
ers, live-wells to keep the fish we catch fresh. It looks as if we are ready to
head off Key West, Florida, for some deep-sea fishing.

"OK, now we need photographs," Tuzee said.

Our completed sport fishing rig is professionally photographed from
every angle. The shot Tuzee likes best is taken from a photo tower. The
entire length of the boat is shown from transom to bow with every piece of
equipment clearly in view. Of course "Johnson" is spelled out across the
transom in foot-high letters.

We send out the press release and photos—including an eight-inch-by-
ten-inch of the full-length photo of the boat—to every daily newspaper in
the Great Lakes area.

◆   ◆   ◆

By now Bill Cullerton and I have become good business associates. We both dig for every bit of information we can find on the Great Lakes salmon phenomenon. I complete a four-page tabloid-size informational piece featuring Johnson Motors, of course, and all of Bill's tackle lines. We mail it to 2,000 daily and weekly newspapers.

There is an urgent need to educate Midwest fishermen about the fantastic new sport fishery that has been created almost overnight. This is big-water sport fishing. It will require bigger boats with larger outboard motors, or the inboard-outboard drives like we have on the "191." Ship-to-shore radios are a good idea for Great Lakes fishing, and that is a very foreign thought to Midwest sportsmen.

This is a sport fishing story almost too good to be true.

On the dark side there are those who have doubts about how long it might last before another evil sea creature makes its way up the St. Lawrence Seaway, finagles its way through the Welland Canal and enters the Great Lakes to once again wreak havoc.

Bill and I meet for lunch in Chicago on a warm summer day.

"We need to plan a fishing trip to Manistee, Michigan, either late this summer or very early this fall," Bill said. "This is going to be the first run of the jack-salmon back up their home streams. Some of these fish could be in the six-to-eight pound class, maybe bigger," Bill said.

I listen in disbelief. Six-to-eight-pound sport fish in the Great Lakes! Unreal.

"Bill, that will absolutely knock everyone over," I said.

"There's no doubt that's what's going to happen," Bill said. "There's going to be more broken tackle, and more people buying heavier gear than in the history of Midwest sport fishing."

"Does anyone else know about this?" I ask.

"Our good friends at the Michigan Conservation Department are watching all of this very carefully. They are certain this is what will occur," Bill said. "Salmon are going to return to the Michigan rivers where they were planted. Before they head upstream they're going to school-up in Lake Michigan right off the entrance to the rivers."

"So, what do we do?" I ask.

"I've already talked with McNally and he wants to go. And McNally said the *Tribune* Sports Editor George Strickler wants to be there," Bill said. "Can you take the Johnson '191' up there and I'll bring along my Lund with the twin-Johnsons."

"I'll be there," I said.

"One other thing. I'm going to ask Jack Bails from the Michigan Conservation Department to join us," Bill said. "He was one of the guys who helped plant these fish."

This is another page from the Bill Cullerton book: Make every event count by including the best people—especially those who bring something extra and professional—to the party.

"That will be quite a group," I said.

"We're going to catch some fairly large salmon," Bill said in a firm voice.

Once we covered the fishing plans, this is an opportunity to find out more about Bill Cullerton.

"I understand you were a fighter ace in World War Two," I said.

"That was in another life," Bill said.

And that was the end of that.

2

Coho Madness

Manistee, Michigan—August, 1967

Four of us gather for an early dinner that August evening in the *home cooking style* restaurant in Manistee, Michigan. We are on the shores of the Manistee River which flows directly into Lake Michigan a half-mile to the west.

Bill Cullerton pulls his big, 18-foot Lund boat with the twin Johnson outboards to Manistee. *Chicago Tribune* Sports Editor George Strickler, and Outdoor Editor Tom McNally fly over from Chicago. And I bring the special Johnson "191" sport fishing rig from Waukegan.

"I'm believing you fellows that we're going to catch some salmon out there tomorrow," George Strickler said.

Gray-haired, rather stocky, Strickler appears to be in his early sixties. He has a very pleasant manner and speaks with that unique, flat Chicago accent.

"George, we're going to catch some salmon tomorrow. I guarantee it," Cullerton said.

"You know, Bill, I've heard a lot of guarantees through the years—usually from coaches," Strickler said. "Not all of them have come true!"

"Is this coming from the same guy who arranged that *Four Horseman* photo in South Bend?" McNally said, peering over the top of his glasses at Strickler.

My ears perk up at that comment. Somewhere I recall having seen a picture of four Notre Dame football players in full football gear, sitting on horses, holding footballs.

"That was a long, long time ago," Strickler said, shaking his head.

"George, that was probably the biggest sports coup of the century," McNally said.

"I was working my way through Notre Dame doing publicity for Knute Rockne. The movie *The Four Horsemen of the Apocalypse* was playing at the rec hall on campus. Must have seen it a half-dozen times. It was the 1924 game with Army at the Polo Grounds. We were tied 7-7 at the half. Everyone was talking about the great Notre Dame backfield. Grantland Rice from the *New York Herald-Tribune* was there and I said something like, 'Yah, like the Four Horsemen.' We beat Army only by 13 to 7. But when I read Rice's lead the next morning, I about fell over," Strickler said.

"Do you remember it?" McNally asks.

"By heart. It's the most famous sports lead ever written," Strickler pauses, looks down at the table and then begins reciting with great feeling: "'Outlined against a blue-gray October sky, the Four Horsemen rode again. In dramatic lore they are known as Famine, Pestilence, Destruction and Death. These are only aliases. Their real names are Stuhldreher, Miller, Crowley and Layden.'"

The hair is standing up on the back of my neck.

"I sent a telegram to my Dad back in South Bend. I said I needed four horses and saddles. When the train pulled in to South Bend, Dad was there and he said he had the horses lined up. They were cart horses from the coal and icehouse company. I saddled them and took them over to the football field. I broke up Rock's practice, put the Horsemen on them, and had the photographer take the picture," Strickler recalls.

"And you owned that picture, didn't you?" McNally asks.

"Yes, I had the rights to it," Strickler said. "Made a lot of money on that picture."

◆   ◆   ◆

We are up at dawn. Jack Bails of the Michigan Conservation Department joins us for a quick cup of coffee. Bails is wearing his official State of Michigan Conservation Department hat and jacket.

Then we are in the boats and head out the Manistee River into Lake Michigan.

Cullerton has McNally in his boat. Bails and Strickler are with me in the Johnson "191."

It is a stunningly gorgeous late-August morning. As we clear the break-water at Manistee, Lake Michigan is absolutely mirror calm. There is no wind, not even a ripple on the surface. In mariner's terms it is "dead calm." We can see for miles to the west, north and south. There are no other boats in sight. It appears we are—once again—the only ones who have any inkling there might be salmon out here.

"So, you're one of the conservation fellows who came up with the idea of putting salmon in Lake Michigan?" Strickler asks, looking directly at Jack Bails.

"I had a small part in it," Bails said modestly. "I work with Howard Tanner and Wayne Tody—and it was really their idea."

"Hell of an idea," Strickler said.

"Yah, it was," Bails said. "We've had 200 million pounds of alewives in the Great Lakes. We've pretty well controlled the sea lamprey-eel. So now we have a chance to introduce salmon with every expectation they will sur-vive through their normal life cycle and hopefully consume a lot of those alewives."

I can see Cullerton and McNally already have their lines in the water. I suggest to both Strickler and Bails it is time to put the Rapalas out and we will begin trolling immediately.

"Holly shit!" I hear McNally exclaim. "Look over there. They're por-poising! I don't believe it! Damn! I should have brought my fly rod!"

Looking off the starboard bow I can see ripples in the water, then splashes—large splashes. The coho salmon are gathering in large schools. And there they are, porpoising. The salmon are swimming along just beneath the surface and then breaking through, roiling the otherwise dead calm water.

Strickler quickly has his line in the water and we begin trolling.

"How long will you be up here?" Bails asks.

"I'm here just today and tomorrow morning. I've got to get back to Chicago by tomorrow night," Strickler said.

We slowly zigzag about a quarter-mile off the Manistee shoreline. Our morning sky is absolutely clear blue, not a cloud.

Suddenly there is action in the Cullerton-McNally boat. We are just far enough away that I can't hear the line screaming off the reel, but I can see the rod tip dip about three feet. Whatever they have on is a big fish. We all watch from our boat as McNally reels…and then the line runs out as the salmon makes another run. After about 15 minutes, McNally raises the rod tip high, Cullerton has the net and they swoop up the biggest fish I have ever seen caught in the Great Lakes.

Cullerton removes the fish from the net and holds it up by the gills. It appears to be about a six-pound, beautiful, bright silvery coho salmon.

"What do you think of that?" Cullerton calls over to us.

"Fantastic!" Strickler replies. "Now, where's mine?"

This is a stunning moment. Lake Michigan—the freshwater dead sea of sport fishing—is yielding six-pound salmon. We have the proof right in front of us when Cullerton holds up the prize.

Jack Bails is smiling from ear-to-ear. Of course he knew salmon of this size were out here. The Michigan Conservation Department had been quietly working off Manistee using big nets to sample the waters

We continue trolling as the sun becomes more intense and takes the chill from the morning air. This is such a perfect day to be out on one of the world's great freshwater lakes.

Twice more we watch as McNally and Cullerton catch large coho salmon. They are having a grand time. McNally tries to remain calm as the salmon makes run after run…and McNally cranks away at his reel time and again…until the big fish finally tires.

I sense Strickler is beginning to wonder if he is in the wrong boat, using the wrong rod and reel, or the wrong bait, or if we are doing something just plain wrong. But he doesn't say anything.

Then with a bang! Strickler's fishing rod bends right down. I cut the throttle back and move the gears to neutral. Jack Bails brings his line in as fast as he can.

For almost 20 minutes George Strickler has one of the great fishing experiences a person can have, fighting a large salmon, slowly wearing down the beast and moving it to the boat.

"I think we're about there," I hear Strickler say.

Jack Bails grabs the net.

I catch a quick glimpse of the silvery flank of a very large salmon coming right up next to the gunwale.

Strickler swoops his rod tip up in the air.

Bails comes around to Strickler's left side, moves the net down into the water and swings the net at the salmon—headfirst.

Well, the big fish just takes one swipe at the rim of that net, leaves the Rapala lure tangled there and takes off for the deep water.

Strickler sinks down in the fighting chair. He is shaking. He drops the rod, drops both hands down past the arms of the seat and said:

"Damn you, Jack Bails, a conservationist to the end!"

And that is the only fish our boat sees all day.

◆   ◆   ◆

We are up again at dawn the next day. Jack Bails leaves us for other chores. After a quick cup of coffee, we are back on our way out the Manistee River toward Lake Michigan.

Nearing the end of the harbor entrance we can see Lake Michigan is not the calm inland sea of the day before. There are six-foot high rollers with a southerly wind blowing whitecaps over the tops of the enormous waves.

Bill Cullerton looks over from his boat and hollers: "What do you think?"

"Forget it," I reply. I turn to George Strickler and said, "Sorry, George. Not a good day for Lake Michigan fishing."

George nods.

Then something straight out from the breakwater catches my eye. Out there are two fishermen in a 12-foot long, square-ended, flat-bottomed, cartopper boat with what appears to be a 30-year-old, three-horsepower outboard motor. They have their lines out fishing for salmon. Huge rollers take them six feet up in the air, and then they totally disappear from our view as they sink to the bottom of the trough between these enormous waves.

"Bill," I call out, pointing toward the apparition appearing and disappearing in the distance. "Do you see that?"

Cullerton shakes his head in disbelief. We turn back to the boat dock.

◆　　　◆　　　◆

Tom McNally's *Woods & Waters* column that following Sunday carries the story of our fishing expedition to Manistee, Michigan. Of course, Rapalas are the fishing lure of choice. And once again there is no mention of my employer, Johnson Motors.

Sport fishermen pick up the million-circulation Sunday *Chicago Tribune* and they read the *Gospel According to McNally*. They load up pickup trucks, station wagons and cars...hitch up their trailers...load their boats and they are off! They stream up the highways on the western side of the State of Michigan, pulling their fishing rigs behind them loaded with rods and reels, coolers, tents...and beer. It is the biggest, strangest continuous parade of fishing tackle laden vehicles ever to roll north. It is like the California Gold Rush and these are the *Miner-Forty-Niners*. This is simply the best thing to happen in Midwest sport fishing in their lifetime. Honest-to-God big fish in Lake Michigan. This is not-to-be-missed.

Coho madness erupts.

From the Sunday that McNally's column appears through well into November there is this crazy quilt, enormous caravan of Midwestern sport fishermen streaming northward on their pilgrimage to catch salmon off Manistee.

The Manistee Chamber of Commerce estimates there are 150,000 sport fishermen in Manistee County, Michigan, during just the month of September, 1967. The United States Coast Guard reports on September 15, 1967, there are 6,000 sport fishing boats in Lake Michigan between Manistee and Frankfurt—a distance of less than 25 miles.

Nothing like it had ever happened before in the history of Midwest sport fishing.

◆　　◆　　◆

Week-after-week passes and there is no mention of Johnson Motors in Tom McNally's *Woods & Waters* column. I am having serious self-doubts about what I am doing, and I am beginning to wonder if my immediate superiors—my boss, in fact—might begin losing faith in my ability to get the Johnson Motors name in print. After all, our job was to help sell Johnson outboard motors and boats.

I pick up the Sunday *Chicago Tribune* on yet another Sunday morning. It is with trepidation I open the sports section to the *Woods & Waters* column.

There it is…the photograph of the Johnson "191" taken from the stern showing the fully-rigged Great Lakes fishing boat. McNally or Strickler—or somebody—had enlarged our eight-inch-by-ten-inch photo! *Enlarged* it! The word "Johnson" screams from the page in letters that appear to me to be two-inches high.

McNally's entire *Woods & Waters* column is devoted to the full description of the Johnson "191" and touts that this is the way sport fishing boats should be rigged for Great Lakes salmon fishing. There it all is, Johnson Motors certified and fully approved in the *Gospel According to McNally!*

◆　　◆　　◆

"Wow! This is amazing!" John Tuzee exclaims as he walks in the Johnson Motors office that Monday morning. "Unbelievable!" Tuzee is holding up the page from the Sunday *Chicago Tribune* with McNally's *Woods & Waters* column. "Fabulous, absolutely fabulous!"

I guessed I could keep my job.

3

Let's Do A Show!

Chicago—August, 1969

Bill Cullerton and I remain good business associates as I move from Johnson Motors to Zenith Radio Corporation and then on to *Show Business* within a two-year span.

I am assistant director—and later director—of the Chicago Boat Show. The show is in the International Amphitheater at 42nd and Halsted on Chicago's south side. The nearby International Stockyards that made Chicago *hog butcher to the world* is on its last legs. However the pungent odor from the slaughterhouses is imbedded in the bricks-and-mortar of the old Amphitheater.

Cullerton's telephone calls were always welcome.

"Hey, John, congratulations on moving on to the Chicago Boat Show. We'd like to exhibit our fishing tackle with you, what do you think?" Bill asks.

I held my breath for a moment and said: "Bill, we're not ready for you. I'll let you know when we are."

It was a tough thing for me to say. But if I suggested that Bill bring his manufacturers into the Chicago Boat Show of that day, I was pretty sure I might not ever hear from Cullerton again. We are a struggling event, barely surviving.

Then the day arrives three years later we are returning to the new McCormick Place on Chicago's lakefront. I call Bill and tell him we are ready!

We create something called *The Panorama of the Great Outdoors* with live, 20-foot tall pine trees and a small lake. We surround it with Cullerton's fishing tackle exhibits. The *Chicago Tribune* sponsors our trout fishing pond where thousands of Chicago area kids catch their first trout. McNally even mentions us in the *Woods & Waters* column! It is a huge success.

Each year we also produce a major international trade show for manufacturers of products in the pleasure boating industry to exhibit their wares to 30,000 dealers and distributors from all over the world. Bill Cullerton is a major influence on any product that is shown that has anything to do with sport fishing. Bill brings his entire staff down to McCormick Place for the run of the event.

◆　　　◆　　　◆

Then I receive the strangest telephone call ever from Bill Cullerton.

"Hey, John. WCFL-Radio wants me to do an outdoors radio show for them," Bill said.

"Bill, that's terrific. I hope you said you would do it!" I said.

"Well, I told them I would do it if *you* would produce it," Bill said.

"Bill, you're crazy," I said. "I've never produced a radio show in my life. I don't know my way around a radio station studio. What are you thinking?"

"No, I'm not kidding," Bill said. "Think about it. I'm on a 50,000-watt radio station talking every day to my customers in five states! If you'll produce it, I'll do it."

"I don't know," I said.

"Tell you what, let's meet with Bill Lemanski, the station manager, and we'll talk," Bill said.

There are five 50,000-watt mega-candle, high-powered radio stations in Chicago. There are only 50 of them in the entire United States. WCFL-Radio is one of those five Chicago stations pumping out a signal that can be heard daytime in at least five states and part of Ontario, Canada, and at night in 23 states and half of Canada. This is what is known in radio parlance as "A Big Signal." However, WCFL-Radio is at the bottom. Owned by the AFL-CIO Labor Union, it had done a big switch from rock-and-roll to something called "beautiful music." The switch is a gross failure.

For two years I produce Bill Cullerton's *Outdoor Show* on WCFL-Radio. I do it on my lunch hour.

Mercifully, the big radio station in Chicago—WGN—"hires Bill away" from WCFL and Bill hits the truly big-time in Chicago broadcasting. For the next 20 years Bill's one-hour *Great Outdoors Show* beams at 6:00 a.m. Saturdays to one-third of the United States and half of Canada. One-half of the radios in the Chicago area are permanently set to WGN-Radio. There was no way I was going to get up at 3:00 a.m. to drive into Chicago every Saturday morning to produce Bill's WGN show. WGN had a corral of full-time professional producers who would do the job.

◆   ◆   ◆

In 1979 we have the opportunity to start our own business producing trade shows and public events and we are looking for stockholders.

One of the events we have in mind is a new show to feature sport fishing.

Bill Cullerton becomes a stockholder, and an exhibitor in what becomes the Chicagoland Sport Fishing, Travel & Outdoors Show held at the O'Hare Expo Center in Rosemont, Illinois, near O'Hare Airport. In the following quarter-century hundreds-of-thousands of Midwest outdoorsmen attend this event, and still do.

In our start-up year I arrange a meeting in the promotions department of the *Chicago Sun-Times*. I am hoping for a few pages of promotional—as in *free*—advertising in return for making the *Sun-Times* our official sponsor.

When I walk in the *Chicago Sun-Times* promotion manager's office, he holds his arms out wide and said: "I've been told whatever you want is yours."

I've never known for certain who made the call, but obviously someone had reached *Chicago Sun-Times* Publisher Marshall Field!

Our company is a huge success. We buy out our stockholders—including Bill—within two years of our founding date.

4

Divine Intervention

May 1988

A year after we sell our company to Capital Cities-American Broadcasting Companies I begin hearing from others that Bill Cullerton is talking about his experiences as a World War Two fighter pilot. The timing is perfect because the money I receive from the sale of the company means I can pursue anything that interests me. And Bill Cullerton's story interests me.

Bill returns to England in May of 1988 for a reunion of his fighter group. He visits the small villages surrounding his old airfield. He meets up—one more time—with his fellow pilots whose friendships were formed in savage dogfights and strafing missions over Nazi Germany.

The reunion jars Bill's memories. Seeing the site of his airfield in England takes him back 45 years. Recalling those days with his fellow fighter pilots makes many of those episodes seem as if they happened yesterday.

Bill Cullerton wants to talk about his experiences in World War Two. Bill's memories are no longer something "from another life."

Perhaps it is now important for Bill to let his five children, and the ever-growing number of grandchildren—is it 12 or 14 now?—know about Bill Cullerton, fighter pilot.

Chicago's WGN-Radio's Roy Leonard invites Bill on his show in June of 1988 and Bill opens up about his days as a fighter pilot. When you talk on a 50,000-watt radio station a lot of folks are going to hear you!

I make an appointment with Bill to talk about his World War Two experiences. Our first meetings are tentative. Bill is talking, but in general terms. I know it is going to take a long time to dig into distant and very personal memories of this tough fighter ace. Bill's memories are vivid and embedded forever. But sharing them is another thing. We tape our sessions over several years. Bill finally tells me things he has never shared before with anyone.

I learn one thing for certain, almost no other human could have survived the war to tell the story Bill tells.

◆   ◆   ◆

Bill and I continue our taping sessions in early 1992.

It is about this time something occurs that approaches what the mystics might call a strange *Divine Intervention*.

My wife and I sold our home in which we raised our children and we bought a Victorian home built in 1892 in Woodstock, Illinois. Along with many, many areas of the home that need help are the original stained glass windows. We try and fail to find professional help. Then we read in the local newspaper that stained glass classes are going to be offered at a local shop—*The Artful Glazier*—on the historic Woodstock Square. Ah! We will take the classes and repair the stained glass windows ourselves. We sign up. After six weeks of classes my wife makes a stained glass piece about one-square-foot featuring a hummingbird. It is a nice addition for our kitchen cabinet door. I make two slightly larger pieces for a china cabinet. I also make a fairly large piece to replace the tacky "refrigerator shelf glass" someone stuck in the lovely original front door.

As the taping sessions with Bill continue, I decide my wife and I need to go over to England to see where Bill Cullerton was based in World War Two.

I call Bill and tell him we are going.

"If you're going over, you need to call the secretary of our 355th Fighter Group Association. Here's his name and number," Bill said.

Minutes later I am talking with 355th Secretary Bob Kuhnert in Dayton, Ohio. Bob knows nothing about me other than that I am a friend of Bill Cullerton's and I am going over to England to visit the group's World War Two airfield.

"I'll send you our newsletter with a write-up about Bill," Kuhnert offers.

The newsletter arrives two days later. In addition to a write-up about Cullerton, there is an item about the upcoming 355th Reunion to be held in England in May of 1993. This would be in honor of the 50th anniversary of the 355th's arrival in England during World War Two. One of the goals of the organization is to raise $25,000 for a stained glass window for a church that was near the base. The proposed window would commemorate the 355th.

I call Bob Kuhnert.

"Bob, I'm an amateur stained glass guy. I'd like to take a look at that window opening and see what I might be able to do," I volunteer.

"You need to right away call David Crow in Steeple Morden. David is our associate who handles everything for us in England," Kuhnert said.

I look at my watch, it is 4:00 p.m. Central Standard Time—meaning it is 10:00 p.m. in England.

I call David Crow in Steeple Morden, England.

"David Crow speaking," he said.

"Right, David Crow. I hope I haven't called you too late in the evening," I said.

"Well, actually, I was just climbing into bed," Crow said.

"You don't have any idea who I am but I just got off the telephone with Bob Kuhnert who suggested I call you," I said. "We're on our way over to England within 24 hours to visit the 355th base. I understand the 355th Association wants to have a stained glass window made for the reunion next year. I would like to see the window in the church where that would be installed."

"Where are you staying in England?" David asks.

"At a bed-and-breakfast in Cambridge," I said.

"When you get there, call me. Good night," David said.

And that is the end of the conversation! The man is tired.

◆   ◆   ◆

After we arrive in Cambridge, England, I call David Crow from our bed-and-breakfast. David arranges for the Church Warden Pamela Sharp to meet us at the bus stop in nearby Litlington.

Pamela greets us warmly and takes us straightaway to St. Catherine's Church, not more than 100 feet from the bus stop.

From the outside St. Catherine's Church appears quite old, but does not reveal its true heritage.

We enter through the massive old-plank door with its hammered iron hinges.

"I'll apologize right now," Pamela said. "This is a very old church and we have some roofing work going on at the moment so things are not as tidy in here as they might otherwise be."

Pamela points to her right as we walk up the center aisle and said: "Over there in the left hand jamb of that second window there is graffiti believed to be from the crew of Sir Francis Drake."

We try to absorb that bit of information. Sir Francis Drake. Our explorer history is not as sharp as it might be.

"Is there a date?" I ask.

"Yes, it is dated," Pamela said. "1595."

Pamela escorts us through the wood-and-glass choir screen and into the choir area, right up to the altar.

"I understand you do stained glass work?" Pamela asks.

"I'm strictly an amateur," I reply.

"Well, here is the window opening we hope to have filled with the 355th tribute," Pamela said, pointing up at a very large window opening. "This part of the Church dates from the twelfth century and we believe this window opening is from somewhere around the fifteenth century," Pamela said.

It takes a moment for that to set in. The window opening we are looking at pre-dates Columbus' first journey to America! Parts of this area of the Church are 900 years old.

The window appears to be at least 10 feet high and almost as wide, made up of three perpendicular openings topped with elaborate stone tracery. It is filled with rather small—not more than four inches on-a-side—diamond-shaped pieces of glass set in lead came. There are scattered spots where pieces of glass have been haphazardly replaced. The original glasswork disappeared long ago. Maybe Cromwell and his cohorts took hammers and axes and destroyed something "Papist." Or perhaps weather or age were the culprits.

"I can do this window," I said quietly.

"You're crazy!" my wife said.

I have no idea why I thought I could make a window of this scope. Achieving success on such a scale was far beyond any capabilities I had demonstrated in the stained glass craft. I have no idea what possessed me to say, "I can do this window." It must have been a flash of something the mystics call *Divine Intervention.*

I then explained to Pamela Sharp that I intended to do the window and give it to St. Catherine's Church in honor of the 355th Fighter Group.

Pamela looks as confused as I had about the Sir Francis Drake graffiti.

◆   ◆   ◆

Tall, lanky, smiling David Crow greets us as we emerge from St. Catherine's Church.

"Right. Now you have seen the Church, let's go to my house for lunch," David suggests.

We thank Pamela, and off we go with David.

"So, what do you think of St. Catherine's?" David asks.

"An incredible place," I reply. "Ancient."

"It's that all right," David said. "And what about the window opening for the 355th memorial?"

"I can do it. I can make the window for that opening," I reply.

"You intend to make the window?" David asks.

"Yes, and give it to the 355th and St. Catherine's," I reply.

David Crow is speechless for a moment.

"Right. How about some fish-and-chips and some white wine—not German white wine. Bill Cullerton won't drink German wine, will he," David said.

Over the fish-and-chips and wine we learn David Crow was a six-year-old when Bill Cullerton was flying from the Steeple Morden Airfield near the Crow family residence. David and his friends would stop at the main entrance to the Steeple Morden Airfield on their way to school and watch the show as Mustangs zoomed into the air en route to *The War.*

"It was the most incredible experience in the world," David said. "Here it was, right in my backyard."

David recalls meeting the 355th Fighter Group ground crew members and having them on one occasion take him into the chow line at the mess hall. Britain was on wartime rations and food was limited, especially sugar.

"They had canned—or what we call *tinned*—peaches. I had never seen such a thing," David said. "They were very good."

David Crow was so impressed by the Americans that when his teacher asked in class one day: "What do you want to be when you grow up?" David's hand shot up: "Please, Mum. I want to be a Yank!"

PART II
The Bulletproof Ace

5

You'll Never Be A Pilot

Chicago, Texas & Kansas—Autumn 1943

Bill Cullerton is the 10,000th to join the Army Air Cadet program in Chicago. He is given the "keys to Chicago" for a couple of days-and-nights.

Then Bill takes the written test to become a cadet.

Bill meets with the cadet training counselor who says to him: "You've written down here you want to be a pilot. We have to give you a shot at being a fighter pilot. But as an experienced counselor, I'm here to tell you that you scored 70 on the test, the minimum qualifying score. There's no way you're ever going to become a fighter pilot. I think what you should do is become an officer."

If the counselor is attempting to dissuade Bill Cullerton from trying to become a fighter pilot, he has taken the wrong tact. Bill takes a deep breath and digs in his heels. Bill doesn't care about being an officer. He wants to be a fighter pilot. All he cares about is flying. Who cared if you were an officer. Nobody cared.

"You should be a bombardier, that's what you should be. That way you'll be a second lieutenant and you'll have a great life," the counselor said.

"No. If I've got a chance, I want to go for fighter pilot," Bill said.

"If you wash out trying to be a fighter pilot, you'll be an aerial gunner instead of a bombardier and you'll never get to be an officer. If you go to flying school and you wash out, that's what's going to happen," the counselor advises.

"No. I want to try fighter pilot school," Bill insists.

◆   ◆   ◆

A defiant Bill Cullerton enters the United States Army Air Force fighter pilot cadet training program.

As Bill progresses through a series of training bases in Texas and Kansas, each base seems more remote from civilization than the last.

Flying is second nature to Bill—academics are not, especially advanced mathematics. To keep up with the math classes Bill takes a flashlight to the bathroom and sits on the stool studying math through the night.

At 5:00 a.m. the cadets are up for their morning run.

There is constant hazing meant to see if the cadets can *take it*. Bill is made to hang from a doorjamb by his fingertips for 15 minutes until he is ready to burst. He is ordered to stand in a brace—full attention—and hold it until sweat is dripping off the end of his nose. Then he is told to run carrying buckets of sand…and to run and run and run until he can't stand it. Bill and the cadets are given orders not to break, not to crack. He sees other cadets who refuse to do what they are told. They are thrown out of the fighter pilot training program on the spot. It is all about discipline. Can you *take it?*

For Bill flying is the great part of the fighter pilot training program. He flies every day. The flying is what it is all about.

Flying starts with the small 175 horsepower Fairchild Pilot Trainer-19 with two open cockpits, one right behind the other—the first for the student, the second for the instructor. Bill learns the fundamentals of flying in the PT-19.

Bill advances to the Basic Trainer-13 with a 450 horsepower Pratt & Whitney radial engine. Those who fly the BT-13 don't call it by the company name *Valiant*. They change that to *Vibrator*. The BT-13 has a special feature—it shudders and vibrates when approaching a stall. Bill begins learning aerial acrobatics in the BT-13.

The big jump is to the P-40 *Warhawk* with an 1,150 horsepower engine. Bill thinks when he lifts off in the P-40 he is going to the moon. Real flying begins with the P-40.

One of Bill's flight instructors is a barnstorming pilot from Canada who teaches Bill things about flying an airplane that Bill is sure few humans have ever attempted. Bill can do everything the old barnstormer can do and he can do it instinctively. Oh, there is the detail of learning how to land. Somehow setting that plane back on the ground is not part of flying. Inside loops, snap rolls, skidding the plane, taking the plane in-and-out of spins, flying inverted almost anything that is possible with an airplane in flight comes naturally to Bill. Landing is another story.

"You know, Bill, that was a terrific landing," the old barnstormer-instructor said. "The only problem is you were 20 feet too high."

◆   ◆   ◆

To be a fighter pilot it helps to be a little *wild-assed.* Part of being *wild-assed* is drinking the local bootleg brew.

On Saturday nights for their social highlight of the week whether in Texas or Kansas, Bill and his fellow cadets go straight to the nearest dust-filled, rundown, crossroads town. The better towns have wooden side-walks.

The locals can see Bill and the air cadets coming and they have the best moonshine bootleg whiskey ever brewed ready for the boys! Everyone in these places is a bootlegger including the gas station guy, the bellboy, the grocer…they all have bootleg booze for sale. The bootleggers tell the cadets what sweet booze it is. "The next thing to mother's milk," one of the bootleggers boasts in a Texas drawl.

Bill and the other air cadets are world amateur drinkers. Most of them are 20 years old. If they tried a drink in their lives it might have been a beer sneaked from some parent's stock and consumed surreptitiously in a back-alley.

Moonshine bootleg whiskey Texas and Kansas style is a high-octane, nasty brew that burns on its way down the hatch and leaves a week-long horrible chemical aftertaste.

Girls are all over the place. They are the local girls. The cadets don't have to look for professionals. The local girls are chasing the cadets. The local girls see the cadets as their ticket out of these middle-of-nowhere, destitute, forlorn burghs. The local girls are hoping to marry one of the cadets and get the hell out of town.

Bill and the other 20-year-old *wild-assed* cadets quickly consume the bootleg whiskey and just as quickly become violently ill and try to find their way back to base.

This is what happens on Saturday nights in 1943 and 1944 in the crossroads towns near the fighter pilot training bases in the middle of nowhere in Texas and Kansas.

◆　　◆　　◆

Bill watches the great weeding-out process take place as the fighter pilot training program moves along week-after-week. The sorting and dropping of cadets from the program seems never to end.

Bill signed into the cadet training program to be a fighter pilot. No one signed into the program to be part of a bomber crew. To be a fighter pilot meant you were John Wayne, Tom Mix and Buck Jones all rolled into one. You were it. You were hot-stuff.

One-by-one cadets are dropped from the fighter pilot program. They are called out and shipped off to become bomber crew—maybe a pilot, or bombardier, or navigator or aerial gunner. You could be called out during breakfast, or lunch, or from class. Bill never knows why *that* particular cadet is cut from the program, but they are gone.

Bill is afraid of making friends because when a cadet is called aside and told they are no longer in the fighter pilot program it is hard to take. No one said it, but they all knew it—this fellow wasn't *good enough*. The cadet who is culled from the program is crushed. Bill is afraid he will be next to be called aside and told he is out.

Almost everyone Bill started with is gone. After nine months only three of every 100 who signed up to be a fighter pilot actually become fighter pilots.

How, under those circumstances, when you are awarded your wings can you not feel just a little bit special? Part of your nature to be a fighter pilot is you know you are hot-stuff. You also do not want to have others think you know you are hot-stuff and somehow better. But you know you are! You have to be.

After the most intense nine months of his young life, Bill Cullerton is awarded his wings.

◆   ◆   ◆

High over Florida Lieutenant Bill Cullerton gives the A-36 full-throttle and begins climbing up beside an enormous puff-white, fast-building cumulus cloud. He is powered upward by the enormous 1,325 horsepower Allison engine. Flying up and up next to the clouds he senses the rate of speed of his climb. When he can feel the fighter finally begin losing its upward momentum it's as if he is sitting still. Then Bill rolls the airplane down the side of the enormous cloud. He takes this spectacular solo ride over and over. Everything in the A-36 is preparing Bill for fighting *The War*. The A-36 is the closest thing there is to the latest P-51 Mustang fighter.

On other days Bill flies from Florida's Hillsboro Airfield with a dozen other A-36 pilots. They go up to 10,000 feet over the Gulf of Mexico and do what they call *rat-racing*. This is a form of cat-and-mouse, a game of *I can outfly you and end up on your tail*. It is practice for the aerial combat to come in *The War*. The pilots line up the A-36 fighters in a long thread and then break off to *rat-race* high over the Gulf. For hours they fly through the clouds, around the clouds, over the clouds, diving and climbing to out-fly the other guy and get on his tail. Day-after-day they *rat-race* to perfect the skills they will need to kill the Nazi bastards in *The War*. Bill practices all of the old barnstormer's tricks until he is on the other guy's tail nine-times-out-of-ten. Still not good enough. The *rat-racing* continues.

At other times the now fully-certified hot-stuff pilots spend hours practicing formation flying, grouping in flights of four with two leaders and their wingmen. This is the classic battle formation they will be using in the very near future as they take on the Luftwaffe fighters.

6

D-Day & June 7 Disaster

Steeple Morden—June 6, 1944

Bill Cullerton boards the Queen Mary in New York harbor on his 21st birthday, June 2, 1944. He disembarks in Gourock, Scotland, the morning of June 6, 1944, and is then on the most beautiful train he has ever seen. The interior is elegant with warm-toned, wood paneling and brass fixtures everywhere.

Rolling through Scotland, down through the English countryside toward Cambridge, all Bill sees out the train windows is green … green … lush green.

While on the train he hears the first word that this is the day—D-Day. The invasion of Hitler's *Fortress Europe* is on!

As he joins other replacement pilots, mechanics, cooks and others on a truck for the last part of their journey from the United States to their assigned bases, it appears every air base is working at full tilt. Steeple Morden is no exception.

Bill Cullerton takes his first glimpse of the Steeple Morden Airfield, home to the 355th Fighter Group, 8th United States Army Air Force. Trucks and jeeps are racing about. It appears everyone is working at maximum effort.

Bill peers across the field at the P-51 Mustangs as they dive to land. Bill sees something different—each plane has wide, black-and-white stripes painted around each wing and around the fuselage. He later learns this is to clearly identify *the good guys*. Allied air power hammers the Nazis day-after-day and achieves what is called air superiority. There are still Nazi planes around—a lot of them—but the Allies can provide sufficient air defenses to keep them away from the Normandy beaches. Allied troops landing on D-Day are told if they see airplanes overhead "they will be ours." To be certain of avoiding friendly fire, the black-and-white stripes are added to leave nothing to doubt.

Bill notices one other thing. As the Mustangs roll down the runway they disappear. After a few seconds they reappear on the other end. The damn runway has an enormous dip in the middle. Bill knows for certain he's not in Kansas.

◆   ◆   ◆

Bill reports for duty at the Steeple Morden Airfield and is assigned to the 357th Squadron.

A forlorn looking pilot Fred Ramsdell shows Bill to his quarters. Ramsdell's deep-set, blackened, no-sleep eyes make him spook-like in appearance. It is as if Charon has arrived incarnate to ferry Bill across the River Styx. It is an unsettling moment. Most of the time in training Bill sensed he was surrounded by comrades in arms who were on a march to victory. On rare occasions, such as this, there is a fleeting moment of doubt. He is 4,000 miles away from home. He misses his family and his girlfriend Elaine Stephen—all her good friends call her "Steve."

Pilot Ramsdell's coal-black eyes buried in this deep furrow beneath his forehead are really bothersome.

The barracks are spartan. Built of dark steel walls with windows along the top and a single potbellied stove, the rectangular room houses a dozen cots on either side of a center aisle. Beds are all made and no one is there.

As Bill and Ramsdell walk to the back of the room a small door opens and a figure emerges.

"Sergeant Booth, meet Lieutenant Cullerton," Ramsdell said.

"Sergeant Booth looks after the place for us," Ramsdell said. "He has an uncle who's a general so be nice to him."

Bill immediately grasps that Sergeant Booth is going to be an important person in this new life in England. The Sergeant appears to be well into his thirties, older by a decade at least than almost everyone Bill has seen on the base so far.

"In case you're wondering, the good Sergeant here is a career Army man who knows the ropes," Ramsdell said.

"Sir, the second cot in from the door on the right side is yours," Sergeant Booth said.

Bill puts his trunk at the foot of the bed. It will remain there, unpacked for several days. Although no one tells him, Bill Cullerton is going to be in an accelerated orientation program.

◆   ◆   ◆

Bill Cullerton is in full flight regalia as he listens to the briefing in the headquarters Quonset. A huge map covers the wall behind the stage. There is England, and to the right is the German occupied Continent. The area around Normandy is highlighted with arrows. It will be the job of the 355th Fighter Group this June 7th to interrupt any German reinforcements moving toward the Allied invasion beaches. Specific instructions are given to each of the three squadrons as to the area they are to cover.

As they leave the briefing for the jeeps that will deliver them to their P-51s, one of the veteran pilots Les Minchew, pulls Bill aside.

"Look, all you need to do when you come back to base is line up your left wing on the church tower on the northeast end of the runway, straighten up and you will be right on the runway—home," Les said.

"There are a lot of churches out there," Bill said. He saw at least two around the base, one not all that far from his hardstand. On the way to the base yesterday he saw dozens of country churches, all very similar in appearance.

"The one you're looking for is on the northeast corner of the field. I doubt you'll see any signs on it, but it is St. Catherine's," Les said.

◆   ◆   ◆

Bill Cullerton feels comfortable in the cockpit of the P-51 Mustang. All the controls look familiar enough, even though the closest he has come to the P-51 in training in the States was the airplane's immediate predecessor the A-36.

Bill's assignment this day is to accompany the squadron as far as the English Channel, then return. He is on an orientation flight to become familiar with the P-51 and with his new environment. It is a first step. He will learn how to takeoff with the group and find his way back to base.

Bill is not told he is in a greatly accelerated flight orientation scenario. The 355th Fighter Group needs pilots, and needs them *right now*.

Each of the three squadrons comprising the 355th Fighter Group is supposed to have 24 P-51s. At full strength the 355th Fighter Group could theoretically put 72 P-51s in the air.

The hard reality is the 355th is losing pilots at a rapid rate. From the group's arrival in England in July of 1943 until Bill's arrival, the 355th has an almost 100 percent turnover with 70 pilots lost in action.

Four replacement pilots are arriving each week, not enough to offset the mounting losses and keep the 355th at full strength. In addition, some of the veteran pilots have flown their required number of missions—and survived—and are returning to the States.

When the 355th arrives in England, the P-47 Thunderbolt, affectionately known as the "Jug," is the first-line fighter aircraft. "Jug" is short for "Juggernaut" a sobriquet pilots give the rugged P-47. There are legends about Thunderbolts being flown back to home airfields from battle with entire chunks shot out of the 18-cylinder, air-cooled, 2,000 horsepower Pratt & Whitney supercharged engine. Pilots love their "Jugs." With their eight .50-caliber Browning machine guns, pilots see these fighters as incredible platforms for delivering death and destruction.

The Thunderbolt's big shortfall is that it lacks the range to provide bomber escort deep into Germany. Even when outfitted with external fuel tanks, the P-47 cannot provide fighter escort to Berlin—a major target of

Allied bombers. Nazi fighters know this and they wait until the Thunderbolts are at their range limit and turning around for home. Then the Nazis pounce on the Allied bombers. Each bomber that goes down in the daylight raids, goes down with 10 American crewmen.

In March the 355th begins receiving P-51 Mustangs to replace the Thunderbolts. By the time Bill Cullerton arrives the 355th Fighter Group is completely outfitted with P-51s. With external fuel tanks, the Mustangs can provide long-range bomber escort for 1,850 miles. With long-range P-51 fighter escort for the bombers the air war over Germany changes.

As Bill Cullerton is waiting for takeoff on his first orientation mission he feels invincible in the P-51 cockpit. He hears the roar of the giant V-1650 Rolls-Royce Merlin engine built under license in the States by Packard. He knows he is in the best fighter plane in the world. He also knows he is hot-stuff. And he knows he is plenty afraid! There is a lot that can go wrong at any moment. What if he screws up? These other fellows out here—20 or more of them—have done all of this many times before. Some of them are aces having destroyed five-or-more Nazi planes. He feels very humble, very unknowing, very afraid. The others are crossing the Channel going to *The War*.

Bill is going to fly back to base—back to Steeple Morden—by himself.

Now Bill looks off to the side and waits for the person on the ground to wave him forward. His P-51 nose tilted up so steeply in front of him he can't see the ground in front of the airplane. Directions for takeoff are given by hand-signals from ground crew. And there it is, he is waved forward for takeoff!

If this were truly a combat mission for Bill, he would have been the wingman and he would have taken off in tandem with the lead pilot. This time his is the only airplane on the runway. With his left hand he eases the throttle, gently. Too much throttle and you could tip the high-powered P-51 right on its nose with the propeller grinding up the runway. Gently. Then as he begins rolling down the runway, more throttle and…up.

Directly ahead Bill can see a full flight of four P-51s from the 357th Squadron. He is to fly behind those four airplanes.

Bill moves the throttle back as the group climbs and begins a sweeping turn to the southeast—to the southeast in the direction of *The War*. He focuses on staying where he is supposed to be with the four-Mustang flight directly ahead of him. They close with the full 357th Squadron. Bill doesn't want to take his eyes off his flight, but a glance makes it seem to him they are short of the 24 Mustangs needed to make up the full squadron. He is not certain how short.

They are over water, over the Channel. Bill was told there would be no radio contact. When he sees the water he is to turn and head back to base—back to Steeple Morden. For Bill this is strictly an orientation flight. He is to look around and familiarize himself with landmarks from the coast back to Steeple Morden.

Bill feels a strange, empty feeling watching Mustangs of the 357th—*his* squadron—heading off to *The War* and he is turning back to base.

Visibility is unlimited. He has the coordinates for Steeple Morden, and he has his radio.

Bill sees a major city off to the north. That has to be Cambridge. He swings southwest. He sees a major airfield—that has to be Bassingbourn, the big bomber base—on his right to the west. Then he spots the Steeple Morden base. There is the church tower. He swings the Mustang around, lines the left wing on the church tower, squares to the runway and he is home.

The Steeple Morden landing strip is a new experience for Bill. It is not a flat field. When he lands from the northeast, he rolls down the runway and dips out of sight before coming up again on the southwest end. From that point it is a simple matter for Bill to taxi—rather steeply downhill—to his hardstand located in the far southwest corner. From Bill's hardstand, bordered by big trees, one might think they were in the northwoods of Wisconsin where Bill used to be a fishing guide during the summers of his high school years. The airfield with all its hustle-and-bustle is up over the hill, out of sight.

Bill's Crew Chief Jerry Seidl is waiting as Bill brings his plane to a stop and shuts down the engine. He has already pulled back the canopy. Seidl is up on the wing.

"How was it?" Seidl asked.

"What an aircraft!" Bill exclaims. "It ran perfectly. You do good work."

"We'll make sure it keeps running that way," Seidl said. "By the way, what are you going to call your mount?"

Bill's big identification symbol is already on the P-51. Designation for the 357th Squadron was "OS." Bill's Mustang was the "OS-X." Those are painted in two-foot high, large black letters on both sides of the body of the airplane.

"We'll call her the *Miss Steve,*" Bill said. "That's spelled s-t-e-v-e. That's what everyone calls my girlfriend. It's short for her last name—Stephen. We'll call her the *Miss Steve.*"

◆   ◆   ◆

As Bill Cullerton fulfills his mission and returns to base, the aircraft of the 357th Squadron continue on their assignment to Chateaudun, France, not far from LeMans. This is a bombing and strafing mission. The P-51 can carry two 1,000-pound bombs if it is not carrying external fuel tanks.

The 357th Squadron spots a convoy and immediately strafes it. They see a train and go after that.

Lieutenant Thomas Foster's bombs hit the ammunition train, which explodes sending chunks of the train along with shrapnel hundreds of feet into the air, shredding the P-51 and killing Foster.

Then Lieutenant Harwood Harrell's Mustang is hit by flak while strafing and he belies in near Chateaudun. Harrell is fortunate enough to evade and with assistance from the French underground returns to Steeple Morden in August.

Things turn really sour for the 357th. A flight of three P-51s is on-the-deck strafing when it is spotted by 15 German Focke-Wulf 109s. The 109s shoot down three of the 357th Squadron's Mustangs. Killed are Lieutenants John Guerrant and Nils Holman. Lieutenant Walter MacFarlane bails out of his shot-up Mustang and becomes a prisoner-of-war.

It is the worst day in the history of the 357th Squadron with the loss of five P-51s and five pilots.

In addition to the misfortunes of the 357th Squadron, the 354th Squadron loses one P-51 when Lieutenant Bob Couture's Mustang is hit by flak. Couture bails out, survives and evades, returning later to Steeple Morden.

It is a very dark day back at Steeple Morden.

If the 355th was short pilots before June 7, it is now critically short of pilots. It will take two weeks of new pilot arrivals just to replace the pilots lost in this one day.

Airplane replacements, parts, ammunition and fuel arrive without interruption. United States' war production is something to behold. Hardware simply floods into the Steeple Morden Airfield. It seems it is more difficult to train fighter pilots than it is to build P-51s.

Word of the losses spreads quickly.

To the 1,700 armorers, mechanics, crew chiefs, radio personnel, cooks, fueling operators and all support staff—the 355th Fighter Group Team—a loss here and a loss there was fairly routine. But to lose six Mustangs in one day with three pilots known killed and three more missing is tough to take. Even the veterans with 10 months of witnessing the combat losses struggle with the June 7 disaster.

For newly-arrived pilot Bill Cullerton it is a shock. He has been at Steeple Morden Airfield almost exactly 24 hours. Here were six guys his age, trained just as he was trained to fly the best fighting machine in the world. This morning they were 21 and 22 year-old hot-stuff pilots. And this afternoon at least three of them are dead. Who knows where the other three are.

Bill's answer to this is to learn everything he can from it. What did those pilots do wrong? Someone, somehow was in the wrong place at the wrong time. Talk with those pilots who returned and find out what they think went wrong. And that's what Bill does.

Maybe it was to drown their sorrows, build their courage, or numb themselves but every pilot who could make it to the 355th Officers Club is there the evening of June 7. The 357th Squadron pilots arrive very late following their second mission of the day.

To his surprise, the senior pilots—those who have survived numerous missions and are still alive to talk about it—are more than happy to tell Bill everything they know. Those senior pilots are aware the best way to help themselves is to help the new guy to be as good as he can be. They want all the help from fighter pilot Bill Cullerton they can get. There is real camaraderie among the pilots. It is a bond made strong by each of them knowing they hang their hind-end over the line every time they fly over German-occupied territory. When they are on a mission they only have each other. There is nobody else out there. You hope like hell everyone on your side is hot-stuff, highly skilled and a deadly shot.

The really good pilots are quite certain they are *bulletproof.* If they know enough, study in detail where the guys who are gone made their mistake, then they can learn to avoid those mistakes. The hot-stuff pilot would skate right through this entire deal unscathed. Those fighter pilots who have been fortunate enough to survive their tour-of-duty long enough to study this deadly game all come to the same conclusion: In order to remain *bulletproof* you have to be as aggressive as all hell. You have to be a hot-stuff fighter pilot. And you have to avoid being at the wrong place at the wrong time.

7

First Combat

Over France—June 1944

On June 17, only 11 days after arriving in England, Bill Cullerton is in the cockpit of the *Miss Steve,* ready for takeoff on a bomber escort combat mission over France. He will be Les Minchew's wingman and they are on their way to *The War* to rendezvous with B-24 bombers over Le Mans at 8:40 p.m.

The *Miss Steve* with its V-1650 Packard-Merlin engine is running smoothly as Bill moves from his hardstand, up the hill to the runway. Ground crew motion him forward for takeoff. Quickly airborne he can see Les Minchew immediately off to his left.

In minutes they are over the English Channel, and a few minutes more they are over France.

Bill takes quick glances at the green fields of France. His eyes are fixed on the tail of Les Minchew's airplane. Bill is not going to screw up. His job is to protect Les. Bill occasionally glances in his mirror, designed to give him a wide-angle view of what is happening behind him. There is nothing there but sky.

Twenty Mustangs of the 357th Squadron are humming along at 300 miles per hour, cruising toward Le Mans at 15,000 feet above France.

There is no radio contact. Perfect silence. That is the way it is supposed to be. Don't give any radio signals to let them know you're around.

The instructions at the briefing were clear. They are to meet up with the returning bomber groups and escort them back over the English Channel. When the leader spots the bombers, he is to sweep around them and above them looking for any German fighters.

Bill realizes Les Minchew is in a wide-arcing turn. Bill remains focused on Minchew's tail.

They fly on for a long time and Bill sees they are over water. They begin a slow turn back toward Le Mans to pick up a second group of bombers.

It seems to Bill they have barely left Steeple Morden when they all are swooping back over the field, swinging around and coming in next to the church tower heading for the runway.

"What'd you think, Bill?" Les Minchew asks.

"All I saw was the hind-end of your plane," Bill said.

"That was a complete milk-run. Boring," Minchew said.

◆　　　◆　　　◆

There was nothing boring about the 357th's mission three days later on June 20th. That evening there is a dull roar as the crowd in the 355th Officers Club in the large Quonset continued to build. Everyone is there—every pilot, every officer from the headquarters staff. And they are celebrating.

This day is a *get-even* day for the disasters of early June.

On this day, the 355th Fighter Group destroys 13 Nazi fighters with no losses to the 355th. In addition, the 355th becomes the third fighter group in the 8th United States Army Air Force to reach the record of having destroyed more than 300 Nazi planes.

Bill Cullerton, drink in hand, spots his leader Les Minchew.

"That was quite a day!" Les said to Bill.

"Yes it was," Bill replies.

"Did you see that 109 I nailed?" Les asks.

"You got a 109?" Bill asks.

"You mean to tell me you didn't see that bastard go down!" Les exclaims. "I nailed him."

"Les, the only thing I saw was your hind-end and my mirror," Bill said.

Mild-mannered in appearance, Alabama born and bred, Les Minchew thinks for a moment about what Bill just said.

"You know, Bill, you were doing the right thing," Les said. "You were keeping those SOBs off my tail. But if my hind-end was all you saw, you missed a hell of a show."

"You know, it was a little like going to my first hockey game. I don't think I saw the puck until the second half," Bill said.

"Things really do move fast up there," Les said. "But you'll get the hang of it. Did you see how many Me-410s and Me-109s made that pass?"

"I never saw them," Bill admits.

"Hell man, there were at least 75 of them. The Jerries can still put up a parcel when they want," Les said. "They didn't hang around long, but we got three of them including the one I nailed."

Bill Cullerton commits himself in his first missions to not screwing up. There is a good reason the fighters fly in staggered pairs. The lead fighter needs a covering fighter following behind, just off and back of his right wing. If attacked from the rear the lead plane has some cover. It is the wingman's job to fall back and take on the attacker. When the dogfights get hot, pilots begin violent contortions to gain position on the opponent. The tough part of the wingman's job is to stay with the lead fighter. For the wingman to stay where he is supposed to be requires extreme concentration and great coordination.

◆   ◆   ◆

June 24th is another big day for the 355th Fighter Group. They destroy 30 Nazi fighters with no losses. Bill Cullerton is not in the air this day, but he parties with everyone that night! And it is a grand party.

On the morning of June 25th the jeep carrying the coffee from hardstand-to-hardstand is very welcome.

As Bill and the 357th Squadron cross over Dieppe, France, they are attacked by a formation of at least 20 fighters coming directly at them.

Bill's radio is a blur of conversation until someone yells: "Break off! Break off! Friendlies! Friendlies!"

The attackers are the 355th's own 354th Fighter Squadron. No one is hit. And the rest of the bomber escort mission is without incident.

There is chatter on Bill's radio as the 357th Squadron returns to Steeple Morden.

"Someone was where they weren't supposed to be."

"Would appear so."

"We came in over Dieppe, right on schedule."

"Right place, right time."

The 355th intelligence officers listen in to the radio chat to have an advance idea of what happens on the missions. They later debrief the pilots.

The radio chatter continues.

"Would it have counted if I'd shot down five of them?"

"Why not, Ace."

And on it went.

Then someone concludes those guys from the 354th Fighter Squadron owe the 357th a few pints at *The Crown*.

The 355th Fighter Group base is surrounded by small villages and each village has two or three pubs. One favorite pub is *The Crown,* located directly across the street from St. Catherine's Church in Litlington. It is a cozy, warm place with low ceilings and a fireplace.

That evening everyone from the 357th and the 354th Fighter Squadrons pours into *The Crown* and the drinking of pints goes on into the night until "last round" is called and all is forgiven.

8

London & The Scot

In the five weeks since his arrival at Steeple Morden Airfield, Bill Cullerton flies 13 combat missions. There is a big push on for the United States Army Air Force to do everything possible to ensure the success of the D-Day landings in Normandy. By July 13 Bill is due for break—a two-day pass.

Bill and his pal Charlie Badavas take the train to London and enter the first pub they find and start drinking. Neither of them drank before they entered the service. Bill's first rounds of alcohol are shots of that nasty bootleg whiskey in those dusty crossroad towns in Texas and Kansas during training. The drinking picks up upon arriving in England. There are drinks at the Officer's Club, pints in the pubs, and shots of brandy during intelligence debriefing after combat missions. Once in London, both Bill and Charlie load up on the drinks. They are soon both drunk when they pick up two English girls.

England is awash with pretty, fresh-faced, well-turned-out young women. The young Englishmen are in the armed services stationed all over the world. The Yanks are in England.

The girls know a better place they can go, so Bill, Charlie and the two girls climb in the back seat of a London cab—a tight fit—so the girls are sitting on the fellow's laps.

"Come on Yank, give me a kiss!" the girl says to Bill.

Bill wants to kiss her in the worst way, but he is very ill. He is sick, drunk, and about to throw up. Bill's hand is over his mouth.

"He won't kiss me! He won't say anything. Let's get rid of these bums!" the girl said.

Bill is trying frantically to get the cab driver's attention to have him pull over. Bill can't seem to get anybody to do anything. The situation is becoming alarming. Finally the cab pulls up at a traffic light. Bill dumps the girl on the floor, opens the door and throws up.

"What in the hell did you do to her?" Charlie asks Bill.

Then Charlie realizes Bill is sick.

The girls are gone. Charlie and Bill walk around London for a while trying to sober up enough to decide what to do next. The streets are jammed with thousands of American servicemen all in about the same state as Charlie and Bill.

"You two are sorry looking."

Bill looks up and sees fellow 357th Squadron pilot Harold Spencer.

"Hey, Spence," Bill said. "This is great."

"Cully, you look like hell," Spence said.

The three of them walk for a while trying to sober up a little and then they go into another pub. The pub is full of British soldiers who seem a little edgy in the company of American pilots. The Brits don't seem to care too much for them. It seems to Bill this is a natural kind of *rub thing*. Here are these hot-shot American pilots hanging out in *their* pubs, drinking *their* ale, with *their* women. Bill sees that this particular group of soldiers are big fellows, maybe coal miners. He sees one Scot with kilts and all. The Scot begins talking with Bill and soon the Scot is teaching the American pilots Scottish songs. Everyone in the place is singing and having a great time, getting along just fine.

"Come on Yank!" the Scotsman says to Bill as he takes him up on the dance floor.

The Scot tells the piano player to stop. This big, burly Scotsman has Bill up there and he says: "Me and this Yank can lick any two bloody *limies* in the joint!"

One of the big coal-mining type British soldiers with enormous arms grabs Bill by the throat and pins him against a wall saying: "You want more, Yank?"

"No, no," Bill shakes his head as he's choking.
The American pilots head for the exit.

9

They're On My Tail!

Hildesheim, Germany—August 1944

It seems to Bill Cullerton there is a routine setting in on combat missions. The 357th Fighter Squadron would rendezvous with a bomber group. According to plans made carefully by headquarters command, the bombers zigzag in an attempt to keep the Germans guessing at their primary target. As the bombers begin their run at the target, Bill sees black puffs of flak miles in the distance. It appears the black puffs are merging into a solid cloud of flak. The German antiaircraft guns are setting up a cloud of steel for the bombers to fly through.

Some days German fighters engage the bombers and the 357th Squadron enters the fight. In the early part of July the Germans are not coming up to intercept the bombers Bill's squadron are accompanying. There are moments of excitement. On July 18 Fred Johnson's engine quits over the English Channel and Fred successfully ditches his Mustang in the Channel to become the 357th Squadron's first air-sea rescue customer.

Missions begin to stack up for Bill and each mission gives him more confidence. When they rendezvous with the bomber groups to provide escort, Bill can now take in the entire spectrum of bombers and fighters. The deadly game is completely visible to him. He also knows he is *bulletproof.*

◆　　◆　　◆

At 10:30 in the morning of August 16, near Hildesheim, Germany while accompanying bombers on a mission the 357th Fighter Squadron is attacked by 20 Messerschmitt-109s.

This is Bill Cullerton's 30th mission and he is a flight leader. His wingman this day is J. Dix Riggs. Everyone calls him "Pappy Riggs" because at 28 he is the *Old Man* of the 357th.

When the Me-109s attack, word goes out on the radio: "Drop your babies, and split-S." Bill drops his external fuel tanks, rolls the *Miss Steve* over and heads straight down. You do not want fuel tanks hanging under your wings in a dogfight.

"I've got trouble here," Riggs calls out on his radio. "Dropped one tank, the other won't drop."

"Hit it again!" someone replies.

"I have. Won't drop. Won't drop," Riggs said.

In the P-51 this can be big trouble. The aerodynamics of the short-body, short-wing Mustang can become challenging with one tank gone and one tank still hanging. "Pappy Riggs" goes into a flat-spin and is last seen on his way toward the ground.

Bill Cullerton focuses on the Me-109s, and does not realize he has lost his wingman. There is no one behind him to tell him there are two Me-109s on his tail. He sees tracer fire zipping past him, looks in his mirror and sees two 109s. Bill goes into a hard turn to his left. Bill feels being left-handed is an advantage in this kind of situation. In the *rat-races* he participated in back in his training days, he often lost pursuers by making a hard left spiral. The instincts of the right-handed world anticipate their target will make a right turn. Bill performs better in tight left circles. The Me-109s turn with him, and they stay with him. Bill pulls into a tighter circle. He keeps raising the nose of the *Miss Steve* to slow down to make an ever-tighter turn.

"Does anyone see Pappy?" Bill said over his radio. "Does anyone see OS-X in a tight circle spinning left in a daisy-chain with two 109s on my tail?" Bill asks.

"No, I don't see you."

"No. Don't see you Cully."

"I'm caught in here with a couple of guys right on me," Bill said.

"Don't see you Cully."

In his mirror Bill sees one of the 109s peel off. He turns tighter to keep the other 109 from having a clear shot. The 109 that peeled off comes at him from three-o'clock and fires at the *Miss Steve* as he passes. There is no damage that Bill can see or feel. But something will have to be done…and done quickly. It is time for a barnstormer move.

Bill snap-rolls the *Miss Steve*, pulls up tight and puts her in a slow downward spin. The 109 that had been on his tail realizes Bill is sliding off and the 109 rolls over and powers up in a steep dive to chase the *Miss Steve*. *Miss Steve* is slowly spinning downward and the 109 is at full power. The 109 zips right past Bill. Bill snaps the *Miss Steve* out of the spin, powers up and is on the 109's tail. Roles are suddenly reversed. Bill chases the 109 right down on-the-deck. Bill is dead astern and has a quick, clean shot at the 109. Bill can see his .50-caliber bullets tearing bits out of the German plane. Bill fires a second and third burst and the 109 hits the ground and explodes.

As Bill pulls up he spots the second Nazi fighter that had taken shots at him while he was in the tight circle. The 109 is now trying to sneak away. Bill turns around and goes after him. The 109 makes a banking turn to the left. Bill is banking right down below him and fires. Successfully shooting an enemy plane with your airplane and theirs in banking turns is a difficult maneuver called a *deflection shot*. Bill fires a short burst. Bits of the 109 are flying off. Damaged, the 109 starts down attempting to regain level flight. Bill is now directly behind the 109 and he fires again. Bill sees the 109's canopy come off. Bill can see what looks like little dust marks bursting off the 109 behind the cockpit. Then the 109 rolls over and goes into the ground.

Bill looks around to see where his squadron is and realizes there are dog-fights in every direction. It appears the 357th Squadron has things in-hand, however and there are no immediate calls for help. Bill decides to gain some altitude to further survey the scene. Other P-51s are also climb-ing.

"Did you see Spence nail those two!" someone shouts on the radio.

"Was that you nailing two Cully?" someone asks.

"Got 'em," Bill responds.

The dogfights are over. Score: 357th Squadron 13; Nazis 1—Bill's wingman, Pappy Riggs

As everything settles down and Bill replays in his mind in slow motion what has just happened, his knees begin shaking. He tries moving his legs around. His knees still shake. They shake all the way back to Steeple Morden. They shake when he stands on the ground on his hardstand. He can't stop them from shaking.

"Are you OK, Bill?" his Crew Chief Jerry Seidl asks, obviously noting Bill is shaking.

"I thought I was, but I'm not sure," Bill said.

"We'd better get you over to Doc Walker right away," Seidl said.

The jeep is there quickly and Bill is on his way to the infirmary, knees still shaking.

Flight Surgeon Dr. Walker sees him immediately.

"Looks like you've got the clanks," Walker said.

"What in the hell are the clanks?" Bill asked.

"Well, when you're in a tight situation you keep your nerves all bun-dled up. Then when things lighten up, something gives. In this case, you're knees have decided to help you let off some steam. You, sir, have the clanks," Walker said.

Walker looks him over from head-to-toe and can find no wounds, nothing else wrong.

"Our cure for the clanks is to send you to a very nice British home staffed by women from the American Red Cross. You'll spend a night there, maybe take a walk in a garden, eat great food and converse with some nice women," Walker said. "That is the cure for the clanks."

◆   ◆   ◆

Maybe it is proximity to death and dying, seeing your 21-year-old comrades wiped out in a flash. Perhaps it is hedging your bet with some religious assurance you are *bulletproof.* Whatever the motivation, fighter pilot attendance at church services at the Steeple Morden Airfield is almost 100 percent.

Bill Cullerton's father sent him to Oak Park, Illinois, Fenwick High School so the Dominican fathers could bring some discipline to the young man's life. That experience is Bill Cullerton's religious connection. And it is the Catholic Church Bill adopts at Steeple Morden. That brings him to Father McHugh, or as he is known at Steeple Morden because of his accent—Boston McHugh.

Bill sees Father McHugh when he least expects. Sometimes it's in the Officer's Mess, other times in the village pubs. Father McHugh hangs out often in the village pubs to keep an eye on his boys and attempt to let them not stray too far.

"Bill, would you assist at Mass this Sunday?" Father McHugh asks one night in a village pub.

Bill cannot bring himself to tell Father McHugh he is not Catholic. So he makes up an excuse to not assist at Mass.

"Sorry, Father. I'm flying this Sunday," Bill said.

Father McHugh nods.

"Perhaps in a week or so," Father McHugh said. "By the way, Bill, you never come to confession."

"Oh, I made confession when I was up in Cambridge last week," Bill said. Of course, Bill never said exactly *where* in Cambridge he made confession.

◆　　　◆　　　◆

On August 26 Bill Cullerton takes off in *Miss Steve* on his 33rd mission. Bill takes in the complete picture of what is happening around him in fast action aerial combat.

The 357th Squadron is accompanying bombers south of Antwerp. By 10:30 in the morning the bombers complete their mission and are on their way safely back over the Channel. The 357th breaks off to pursue "targets of opportunity."

Bill surveys the ground below him and spots a Focke-Wulf 200, a big, four-engine German transport plane. Bill puts *Miss Steve* in a steep dive and goes after the Nazi plane. By the time he catches up with it the FW-200 is on the ground at the Speyer Airdrome, Germany, and Bill fires his guns. The FW-200 is still rolling on the runway when Bill hits it and it bursts into flames.

In the debriefing following Bill's return to Steeple Morden the intelligence officers are wondering out loud who might have been on that transport plane. There are reports of a major German general in the Speyer Airdrome area this day, perhaps on the FW-200.

10

Seven In One Day

Schwartz Airfield—September 12, 1944

Bill Cullerton is indoctrinated in the 355th's fine art of strafing ground targets. By June 1944, the 355th has become skilled at this high-risk task.

In early 1944 the German air force begins holding back fighter planes to husband them in hopes of fighting off an Allied invasion of Hitler's *Fortress Europe*. The Nazis are hoping to have enough fighters to attack any beach landing attempts.

If the Nazi airplanes will not come up to fight, they will have to be destroyed on the ground.

Many techniques are devised to attack German airfields. So far, they are not effective.

Dive-bombing seemed to make sense as you are a small target starting from high altitude, dropping bombs, then pulling up level and quickly leaving the scene.

The real trick would be to let the P-51s come in at extremely low-level and use their .50-caliber machine guns to nail parked enemy airplanes. But how to do that without exposing yourself at low-level flight to every gun from pistols to German 88s?

The Top Brass in the 8th United States Army Air Force decides there is a need to develop better ways to strike the German fighter planes on the ground.

In March 1944, several 355th pilots volunteer to learn a new way to strafe ground targets. They attend an instructional course presented by Colonel Glenn Duncan of the 353rd Fighter Group.

The new technique is to approach a German airdrome at an altitude of 15,000 feet. About 20 miles from the target they dive picking up speed to 400 miles per hour. The P-51s are then on-the-deck and about 15 miles from the target. The Mustang squadron flies abreast, as close as they dare to the ground for maximum surprise. On the ground the P-51s cannot be heard until they zoom right overhead. At the critical moment of passing directly over the airdrome at 100-feet off the ground, the pilots point their fighter's nose slightly down and fire.

The 355th Fighter Group masters this technique of ground strafing and becomes known in the 8th United States Army Air Force as the *Steeple Morden Strafers*.

Bill Cullerton becomes a strafing expert.

◆　　　◆　　　◆

As the 355th Fighter Group joins up over Steeple Morden on September 12, 1944, to accompany B-17s on a mission to Brux, Czechoslovakia, Bill again feels invincible. There isn't any German pilot or ground-fire that can hit him. He is *bulletproof*.

All three squadrons are on this September 12 mission and 68 Mustangs are in the air, on their way to *The War* to meet the First Air Division bombers north of Ludwigslust at 10:45. One hour into the mission 40 Focke-Wulf-190s and numerous Me-109s close with the bombers. The 355th goes after them shooting down three German planes.

Bill takes the *Miss Steve* down after the 109s but can't catch them. To Bill's surprise he is right over a German airfield—Schwartz Airfield—and he fires his .50-caliber machine guns as he comes across the field. It is an unreal moment. Bill cannot imagine what the Germans are doing. There are airplanes all lined up in rows with almost no camouflage.

Bill fires the first burst and sees fuel flaming down the side of the first airplane in the row. He watches the first fighter plane blow up and it in turn blows up the next two airplanes in line.

There is nothing to hide now, so Bill comes on the radio:

"We've caught them with their pants down. Hammer them!"

Bill pulls up to go around for another pass at the airfield. The field is surrounded by very tall pine trees, probably over 100-feet in height. As he approaches the field he is not more than 20-feet above the treetops. Then he sees the bastards—a flak station right up in the treetops. He is so close he can see the gunners' eyes. They are not 30-feet to his right and 20-feet below him. Their guns are pointed straight up. He can see the lanyard wrapped in the hand of one of the gunners. The flak gunner's job is to pull that lanyard at the moment an enemy airplane is directly overhead and blow it out of the sky. Bill is too far over to the left for the German to take a shot. But now Bill has spotted them and he isn't going to forget where they are. This is personal war. It is war at eyeball-to-eyeball level. This is the moment to abandon all thought of aerial combat or strafing the airdrome. These flak gun bastards have to die.

Bill abandons his pass on the airfield and wheels around. He stays low and comes in again at treetop level this time spraying the trees with .50-caliber machine gun fire. Bits and pieces of pine treetops are flying everywhere. He has no idea if he hit the bastards on the flak platform or not, but he gives it his best.

Then Bill makes another run at the Nazi fighter planes parked on Schwartz Airfield. They are so neatly in line. Bill squeezes the trigger in a long burst as he flies at 150 feet above the field with *Miss Steve's* nose tipped down. He visualizes that platform he is flying with those .50-caliber machine guns perfectly aligned to shoot up the Nazi fighters.

Bill looks back at the airfield as he and the other pilots from the 357th Fighter Squadron pull away. Black smoke is rolling skyward amongst huge spikes of flame.

Bill's radio is alive with chatter.

"Man, look at that place burn!"

"We pasted them!"

"Anybody see Chapman go in back there?"

"Yah. Flak."

Silence.

When the intelligence officers back at Steeple Morden review Bill's gun film they confirm Bill destroyed seven Nazi fighters. Bill is certain he nailed a bunch more, but he isn't going to argue. All he cares about is the Nazis have a lot fewer fighter planes this afternoon than they had this morning. And he hopes those flak gun bastards are in the ground.

11

The Pub Crawl

English Countryside—1943 to 1945

Bill Cullerton and the other fighter pilots are at a social disadvantage when it comes to meeting the local girls. Not many of the Yank fighter pilots are what anyone would call socially smooth—there are exceptions, of course. Fighter pilots are also at a deficit with the local girls because the other fellows—hundreds of them—arrived first.

Most of the 355th Fighter Group support troops—1,700 of them—arrive in July 1943. They will be at the Steeple Morden Airfield for the duration, however long that might be.

Fighter pilots fly their missions and go back home. That usually means—if you survive—you are at Steeple Morden for not more than five or six months. During that time you fly 50 to 60 missions, not leaving a lot of time for social interaction.

The odds of completing a full tour with the 357th Squadron of the 355th Fighter Group are not good. Of the original 28 pilots in the 357th Squadron who arrive at Steeple Morden in July 1943 only eight come through unscathed. Of the 128 replacement pilots in the 357th, 70 make it through unscathed.

There are many ways to die as a 357th Squadron fighter pilot. You can be killed in air crashes when your Mustang ices up in cold winter sleet and goes down. You can die if you lose your bearings in the unending fog and rain over England. You can stall out for many reasons over the English Channel and hit the water. If you go into the drink at the wrong angle it is like hitting a concrete wall. You can be shot down—usually by flak—and killed or taken prisoner. Or, if you are really lucky you can be shot down and evade the enemy. Those who evade and successfully make it back to base are sent home. The fear is that if you are shot down a second time and captured you will be tortured until you reveal how you evaded the first time. That could expose the Dutch, French and Spanish underground operatives who assist evading Allied pilots.

No one can blame the 357th Squadron fighter pilots if they are a little *wild-assed*. They aren't fools. Even if they are certain they are *bulletproof* they know they are on the wrong side of the odds of living much past the age of 21. Those who survive more than a dozen combat missions see too much. They watch friends go down in balls of orange and yellow flames. There are times you shake hands with the new guy who is a casualty of a first combat mission. It is really tough when a veteran of a dozen or more missions—someone you hoisted pints with a couple of nights before—and you thought was for certain *bulletproof* goes down…your fighter pilot pal and his Mustang shredded into indistinguishable pieces scattered across some beet field in Germany.

On many evenings the *wild-assed* fighter pilots participate in what they call *pub crawls*. Everyone in the 355th Fighter Group is issued a bicycle. Some evenings the pilots pedal off to the first pub they come to—it might be the *Red Lion*—and proceed to have a pint-or-two. Then it is off to the next village to another pub, perhaps the *Fox & The Hound* for another pint-or-two. And so it continues into the night until they can no longer balance on the bicycles and they start walking. There are bicycles scattered all over the English countryside, usually not too far from places like the *Red Lion* and the *Fox & The Hound*.

The next morning after several cups of hot coffee the *bulletproof* 357th Squadron pilots climb into the cockpits of their V-1650 Packard-Merlin powered Mustangs with hundreds of rounds of .50-caliber machine gun bullets and are off to *The War*.

12

Toasting Stalin

Russia & Italy—September 1944

In August 1944 the Polish Freedom Fighters wage open warfare on the Nazi occupation. Bitter, protracted fighting is taking place in Warsaw while the Russian Army "pauses to reorganize" not far from the Polish border. With no Allies coming to their aid, the situation for the Freedom Fighters in Warsaw is desperate.

The only assistance the Western Allies can provide is in the form of air-drops of weapons, food and medicine.

On the morning of September 18, the 355th Fighter Group launches 72 Mustangs to escort the 95th, 100th and 390th Bomber Groups on their way to drop relief supplies to the Polish Freedom Fighters.

This would be a three-part mission. On this day the B-17s would fly over Warsaw and drop food and medicine to the Freedom Fighters. The entire formation would fly on to Russia, land there, reequip and refuel and fly on to Italy. From Italy they would fly back to England.

Following scattered skirmishes with German fighters, Bill watches through the overcast as 107 Flying Fortresses drop tons of supplies over Warsaw.

The 357th Squadron planes find their way through haze and smoke and land on the grass strip at Piryatin, Russia. It doesn't take Bill long to pull out the whiskey and cigarettes he brought along. Every pilot stashed ciga-rettes and whiskey for the Russians. That night at dinner with the Russians Bill toasts Stalin. He toasts Churchill. He toasts Roosevelt. Between the Russian vodka and the American whiskey, the Russians and the 355th pilots are a very soused bunch.

Early the next morning the 355th takes off to escort the bombers on the second-leg of the shuttle mission. The Fortresses are loaded with Russian bombs to hit the marshaling yard at Szolnok, Hungary.

Bombing completed, the 355th makes its way on to Foggia, Italy.

At Foggia there is a barbershop on the base and Bill Cullerton decides it is time for a haircut by a real Italian barber. Bill's thick, black head of hair draws raves from the Italian barber who concludes Bill must be Italian.

"You…you Italian?" the barber asks.

"Yes," Bill answers. His pals back in Chicago's Irish neighborhoods would have enjoyed this. Bill knew his black hair came from his *Italian mother*. Right. Bill's mother was a black-haired Scot whose maiden name was Jamison. Bill's sense of humor was all Cullerton, all Irish.

The barber begins speaking to Bill in Italian.

"One moment. One moment," Bill said. "I have a sad story to tell. My mother and my father would never let me speak Italian at home. So I never learned Italian."

"That is terrible!" the barber said in broken English. "Tragic!"

It didn't matter that Bill could not speak Italian. To the barber *he is* Italian, and that is all that matters. Because *he is* Italian each morning the 355th is in Italy eggs and beer are delivered to Bill's tent.

At 9:59 on the morning of September 22 the 355th takes off on the last-leg of the mission. They escort the bombers to Auxerre and then head for England.

Steeple Morden Airfield has almost zero-visibility when the Mustangs arrive in the area at 5:00 p.m.

"Let's go down a little here and see what we can see," Bill tells his flight.

"F-122 tower do you read?" Bill asks, calling to the Steeple Morden base.

"Yes. Can you see the church tower? Can you see the church tower?" the base radioman calls.

Just then over to his left, Bill spots the tower of St. Catherine's Church.

"Yes. We're home."

◆   ◆   ◆

Food in the Steeple Morden mess looks better than ever after the long shuttle mission. The fighter pilots are very well fed.

As a matter of routine, after landing and taxiing to their hardstands the pilots report to the intelligence officers for debriefing. If the mission was a tough one, they would be served a shot of brandy. If it was a really tough one, there would be a second shot of brandy.

The pilots would then go to the mess and they would dine.

One day Bill Cullerton is seated next to the 355th Flight Surgeon Doc Walker.

"Doc, I sometimes have the feeling I'm being fed like I'm a horse," Bill said. "Look at this. There's meat, stuffing, potatoes."

"It's simple Bill. It's late afternoon. We want you to take a shit about midnight. That way when you're on your mission tomorrow at 5:00 a.m. you won't have to shit in your flight suit," Dr. Walker said.

After the meal, the pilots relax for a little while and then take the footpath over to Litlington, over to the Community Hall in the Congregational Church.

The women of the Village of Litlington have tea, cocoa, biscuits and *hot jam toast* for the Yanks. This is part of the effort the people of the villages make so these Americans feel welcome. It is something to take the edge off their loneliness.

Somehow these *Mums*—as Bill and the others learn the women called themselves—are able to see through the bravado of these Yanks and learn to know them for who they are—lonely young men far away from home and facing great danger. Many of the women think of their own sons and husbands who are on some distant military battlefield, just as lonely, just as scared deep down inside as are these young Yanks. Serving them *hot jam toast* is a way for the women to stay busy and *to do their bit.*

The Yanks love it. They "queue-up" in front of the hall in Litlington. These acts of kindness touch the young men deeply, more so than the women can ever imagine.

13

One Better

The 355th Fighter Group squadrons are airborne at 10:12 in the morning of November 2nd on a "freelance mission to accompany bombers and break off to roam at will seeking Nazi airplanes to destroy in the air or on the ground."

This is the kind of mission any hot-stuff P-51 pilot can enjoy. If you are *bulletproof,* invincible, seated in the best fighter airplane in the world what could be better than to be let off your leash and told—"Go get 'em boys!"

Fifty-six Mustangs from the 355th meet up with First and Second Division bombers at 12:16 just west of the target—Merseburg, Germany.

Bill Cullerton spots two Nazi jets, the Messerschmitt 262s coming from the direction of Berlin. Bill and the 357th Squadron take off after the Me-262s. It is no match. The jets can outrun the Mustangs by close to 100 miles per hour. But the jets burn fuel at a rapid rate and can be airborne for only short periods. The Me-262s are not interested in aerial combat and they dive for the ground. Bill and the 357th Squadron go after them. A P-51 in a dive can hit well over 450 miles per hour. The 262s are long gone, but when Bill pulls up at about 500 feet above the ground he spots a group of Focke-Wulf 190s and Messerschmitt-109s landing at an airdrome near Wernigerode, Germany.

Bill cuts back the throttle, noses the *Miss Steve* down and lines up 300 feet behind a Me-109. A short burst from his .50-caliber machine guns, followed by a second burst and the 109 noses down into the ground. Directly in front of Bill is an FW-190. He fires twice more and the 190 goes down and bursts into flames.

Bill is 200 feet off the ground and right over the airdrome and begins firing as he passes. He powers up to gain altitude, circles and makes another pass…then another.

When the Steeple Morden intelligence officers view Bill's gun film they confirm he destroyed a German Me-109 and an FW-190 in the air and six more fighters on the ground. Once again, Bill is certain he nailed more on the ground than the intelligence guys counted. But who knew? And it really did not matter. Once again the Nazis were short a whole bunch of fighter planes that would not be able to come up after the Allied bombers.

Bill Cullerton is the first fighter pilot in the 8th United States Army Air Force to destroy eight Nazi fighters in one day. Putting these eight together with the seven from September 12 and Bill is also the first to destroy 15 Nazi planes in two days.

◆   ◆   ◆

After the experiences of encountering swarms of Nazi fighters on November 2nd, the 355th Fighter Group makes an all-out effort on November 4th sending up 60 Mustangs to accompany Second Division bombers who are going after the oil refineries at Misburg, Germany Although the flak over Misburg is heavy and one B-24 goes down, no German fighters come up to intercept.

This is Bill Cullerton's final mission.

◆   ◆   ◆

The top brass of the 355th Fighter Group asks Bill Cullerton to "drop by the headquarters before he leaves." They want to have a chat.

Lieutenant Cullerton has completed his tour. He has flown 55 combat missions and a total of 270 combat hours. He has destroyed a large chunk of the Nazi Luftwaffe.

"Bill, if you'll return for a second tour we will make you a flight leader. You know we need the best experienced pilots who can lead. We need you back," Lieutenant Colonel Everett Stewart said.

Here he is with the top brass of the 355th Fighter Group being told he is hot-stuff. This is near the highest rung of the fighter pilot's big ladder. It could not get much better than this.

Bill knows he is *bulletproof.* He also knows he is mad-as-hell at the damned Germans. The pile of Nazi airplanes he has destroyed is a good start, but he can do better. And he has lost too many of his comrades to these Nazi bastards. If he can return and help the 355th Fighter Group destroy these SOBs, he will do it.

The base top brass don't have to bend Bill's arm.

"Sure, I'll come back," Bill said.

14

Welcome Home War Hero

Chicago—November 15, 1944

Bill Cullerton's picture is all over the Chicago newspapers. Here is a genuine *war hero* fighter pilot who sallied forth in single combat to smite the wicked enemy.

Every politician in Illinois wants to stand next to Bill Cullerton and have his picture taken. There is Bill in all the Chicago newspapers beaming, standing with Chicago's Mayor Edward J. Kelly. Mayor Kelly looks as if he is going to burst with pride. He is standing with a real, homegrown, born-and-bred Chicago *war hero*. By the way, this doesn't hurt your chances for reelection…standing next to Bill Cullerton *war hero*.

There is Bill Cullerton outside Chicago's Union Station being kissed on both cheeks by his mother and his girlfriend, Elaine Stephen—Steve. And there is Bill and his mother, sister, father, and Steve all striding up the sidewalk outside Union Station.

It is a triumphant return of the *war hero*.

Bill hopes the counselor at the recruiting depot who told him "you'll never become a fighter pilot" will see the pictures in all the newspapers…and remember.

Now he has to break the news to his family—and girlfriend—he is going back…back to *The War* for a second tour.

PART III

Struggling Toward
A Window

15

Window Designs

Upon returning to our home in Woodstock, Illinois, in March 1992, following our visit to Steeple Morden and Litlington to see the 355th Fighter Group airfield I write to Pamela Sharp, warden of St. Catherine's Church in Litlington, England:

"If you would agree, I would be pleased to do the restoration of the three windows with the addition of a tribute to the 355th Fighter Group. My work would be a contribution to you and the 355th.

"If you wish to proceed along these lines, the first item is to approve the design for the windows. This, of course, is entirely up to you."

I make a very simple design for the window. It is a green wreath with the name "355th Fighter Group 8th USAAF" and the dates the group was in England.

The design purposefully avoids anything *too warlike* or *too American.* Stained glass windows have a way of lasting a very long time in England. Some have survived for a thousand years. The British are the ones who will see this window—in their church—every Sunday for maybe a millennium. We want to make something they will find pleasing.

Secretary, and World War Two veteran of the 355th Bob Kuhnert makes suggestions for reworking the simple design I submitted to him.

First Bob is profuse in his gratitude of the offer of the window for the 355th. It is, in his language "over the top." He has accepted the reality the group cannot raise $25,000 and have the window completed in one year's time.

"Now to the design business. You asked for input, so if you don't object I'll include here some info for you to consider," Bob writes.

Designs fly back and forth from Woodstock, Illinois to Bob's home in Dayton, Ohio. We work and work to come up with something we feel will honor the 355th and not offend the folks of St. Catherine's Church.

In the midst of our design discussions, work and revisions, I receive a letter from St. Catherine's Church Warden Pamela Sharp. It is dated May 4th, 1992:

"Your wonderfully generous offer of replacing the window in our Church amazed and delighted me. Since we met the following has happened...."

Pamela covers the host of meetings and details she has tended to with regard to the window project. There seems to be confusion entering the situation with regard to the window design. It is apparent in reading Pamela's letter they think the window will be designed in England.

Unfazed, Bob Kuhnert and I forge ahead.

When our design work is complete, we have the emblem of the 8th United States Army Air Force at the top of the center window. In the wreath is the wording: "355th Fighter Group, 8th USAAF—July 1943–July 1945." Below that is the 355th's motto: *Our Might Always.*

That's all there is. Nothing *too warlike,* nothing *too American.* It is a simple wreath with symbolic emblems in the upper parts of the windows.

Surrounding all of this is clear glass. This is intentional as this south-facing window provides the major light for the choir and altar areas in the dark winter months in England.

In mid-May, Bob Kuhnert writes:

"I'm excited about the window and your fine design concept. You are most kind to entertain my comments and suggestions. I'm sure the folks in England will be pleased...."

The *final design* for *The Window at St. Catherine's* is carefully packaged and sent by air-mail to Litlington, England.

And then we hear...nothing.

16

Suspicions About Bishop

Ely & Litlington, England—July 1992

Many have likened Ely Cathedral to a great ship. This comparison is for good reason as Ely Cathedral rises mystically from the expansive fen of the vast East Anglian plain. Enormous white stone Romanesque towers jut skyward looking for all the world as if this were a massive tall ship with all sails set gliding over a great marshland.

This is the seat of the Bishop of Ely.

St. Catherine's Church in Litlington is in the Shingay Group of parishes, part of the Diocese of Ely.

In the States among some associated with the 355th Fighter Group it is part of the legend of *The Window at St. Catherine's* that the church members in Litlington forwarded the window design they received from the States to the Bishop of Ely for approval. As events unfold there is a great deal of emotion on both sides of the Atlantic and so there could—possibly—be confusion on this point. Who, if anyone, receives the design at Ely Cathedral remains unknown although there are some in the States who hold it arrived on the Bishop of Ely's desk. Whoever receives the design summarily rejects it.

Some in the States speculate the Bishop of Ely is not pleased at the prospect of a *Yank* making a stained glass window for his church in Litlington. It is a number-one rated church, deemed most worthy of preservation by those who rate such things. No one knows it for a fact that these are the Bishop of Ely's thoughts, but there are those in the States who thought it might be so.

Who could blame one for such suspicion?

The Bishop of Ely has authority earned through *the ages*. Monastic Ely was founded in 673 by the Saxon Queen of Northumbria St. Etheldreda. It was sacked by the Danes in 870 and refounded by the Benedictine Order in 970. Most of the present-day Cathedral was begun by the Normans in 1080. In a high loft of the Cathedral is a stained glass museum showcasing works dating back to the eleventh century. A thousand years of stained glass is not a trifle.

So, a *Yank* is going to design and make a stained glass window to be placed in the altar area of St. Catherine's Church in Litlington! The very window opening selected for the work dates from 200 years before Jamestown was settled in the *New World.*

Perhaps those who wonder about the Bishop of Ely's thoughts on this matter are off-track. Perhaps the Bishop of Ely simply does not like the design of the window as submitted by the *Yank*. Perhaps the Bishop of Ely never saw the design. Perhaps.

There is another exchange of letters that extends into July and then into August.

On August 20th St. Catherine's Church Warden Pamela Sharp sends a fax to Bob Kuhnert:

"Ref design of window, have engaged Alfred Fisher (Chapel Studio, Hunton Bridge, Kings Langley, Herts) specialist glass designer to prepare drawing to present to Bishop's planning committee for approval. Approximate cost is £400 to £500 sterling. He will also produce scale plan for John Dobbertin at a cost of £1,500 sterling approximately.

"Does this meet with your approval?"

Kuhnert forwards the fax to me with a long, personal letter, which basically said this wasn't how he thought the window design was going to be done.

I do some quick math and realize the design estimate is $1,000 with another $3,000 for the scale plan—$4,000 total.

My response is to send a fax straight back which says in sum: "Sorry we seem to have run up against The Church. This was not the way we had intended to do the window."

As Bob Kuhnert accepts our defeat he prepares to tell the Board of the 355th Fighter Group Association that it is very unlikely there will be a stained glass window in St. Catherine's Church for the 50th reunion.

Bob's letter to me concludes: "I extend a sincere thanks for your most generous gesture. We will surely meet eyeball-to-eyeball and hoist a cuppa tea over this episode."

Two days later my telephone rings:

"Hello, John, Bob Kuhnert here."

Bob's voice is now familiar.

"Did you hear the explosion from across the Big Pond?" Bob asks.

"No," I respond.

"Well, your fax was received in England. The Brits are beside themselves," Bob said. "They want that window! We'll be hearing more from them very soon."

I reread Pamela's fax to try to fathom what might change to make the creation of the window a possibility.

The folks in Litlington—or maybe it's the Bishop of Ely—have retained Alfred Fisher to do the window design. I know of Alfred Fisher. His name is referenced as a consultant in a book I admire and is in my library entitled *Stained Glass*. He also happens at this moment to be the president of the Society of Stained Glass Painters. The man has *credentials!*

Alfred Fisher submits two suggested designs to the folks at St. Catherine's Church. On October 1 they arrive in Woodstock, Illinois.

I am shocked when I see the eight-inch by ten-inch color renderings. It is immediately obvious Alfred Fisher intends the selection of the rendering marked "B." Everything in this sketch conveys powerful messages.

Here is the American eagle, wings spread wide across all three window openings. On the eagle's chest is the union jack all red-white-and-blue and set about three-quarters of the way up the center light. Below that is the 355th Fighter Group's coat-of-arms. It is incredible in its brightness. Here is a glistening sword surrounded by flaming red, cutting through a dark-blue background, trailed by a sheet of bright yellow. Below in a scroll is the motto of the 355th Fighter Group: *Our Might Always.* Below that in black letters against a yellow background are the words: *355th Fighter Group, 8th USAAF—July 1943–July 1945.*

Yellows and blues are woven into a grand design highlighting the silhouettes of the P-47 Thunderbolt and the P-51 Mustang.

At the top of the center window is the emblem of the 8th United States Army Air Force, a work of dark blue and yellow with a bright red star.

The window design is a tour-de-force of brilliant colors. Its war symbols scream out at you. It leaves no doubt this is a tribute to American warriors.

I am stunned.

Then I am frightened. How in the world am I going to make this very complex, extremely colorful eight-inch-by-ten-inch rendering into a stained glass window almost nine feet high?

Then I read the accompanying letter from David Crow, chairman of the 355th Fighter Group in the UK:

"I enclose photographs of two designs for the proposed stained glass window. You will see immediately that they have been altered from your original design to be more acceptable to the Diocesan Advisory Committee at Ely, who have to approve any works that are carried out."

Ah, perhaps some suspicions are here confirmed. Perhaps the Bishop of Ely lurks somewhere behind the Diocesan Advisory Committee.

"When you met with Pamela Sharp and me earlier this year we had no idea we had to have official approval, hence the delay. However, we can now confirm that the necessary approvals have been confirmed on either the 'A' or 'B' design.

"We do sincerely hope you like the work and agree that your original design has been enhanced by Alfred Fisher…. It may help you to know that the Litlington Church members and the 355th UK Committee like design 'B' as being the most suitable for the Church…."

If design "B" is what they want, then design "B" will be what they receive.

There is also the matter of securing the correct size of the windows. While looking at the window openings it was very apparent gravity and weather had taken their toll over 600 years. The window sill slanted perhaps three or four inches from one end of the opening to the other, and the window appeared to be several inches out of plumb. The only way to proceed is to have someone in Litlington make stiff paper templates of each of the three lights. This will be a challenging task.

A friend of St. Catherine's Church and a man with a keen interest in architecture Peter Griffiths takes on the task of making the templates. They arrive in Woodstock on January 12, 1993.

In doing the templates Peter makes some disturbing discoveries: "I have had some difficulty with the tops of the windows—the stonework in parts has crumbled away and will have to be renewed, so I have had to guess the exact pattern in those parts. The templates are otherwise the shape of the window as it now is (I hope!). I have made no allowance for any inset into the stonework to support the window. In parts, at the moment, there is no support; in other parts there is a quarter-inch inset. In other parts it is slightly more."

An inch here, a half-inch there can make a huge difference when a stained glass window is set in place. You can't just take a pair of scissors and cut the stained glass window to fit. Peter's observations are bothersome. We must allow a *fudge factor.*

Peter also reports the stonework between the lights is five-and-one-half inches, saying: "I took sample readings at several points on both verticals and they were (surprisingly) all the same to the tolerance I was measuring."

At least something about the window openings is consistent.

The 355th Reunion is scheduled for the weekend of May 16. Allowing 30 days for shipping and installation, there are now 90 days remaining to make the window. There is no time to waste.

To expedite the making of what stained glass craftsmen call the *cartoon,* or master drawing made to the window size, I take Alfred Fisher's eight-inch-by-ten-inch rendering to a computer fellow by the name of Jim Brown. Of all coincidences, Jim's father worked for Bill Cullerton for several years. While that is in progress, stained glass expert Ken West of *The Artful Glazier* accompanies me to the largest stained glass distributor in the Midwest, Hoy's in Warrenville, Illinois.

Hoy's has a 50,000-square-foot building filled with shelves containing stained glass of every quality and color imaginable.

We narrow the hunt by going directly to the very best, most expensive stained glass in Hoy's vast inventory. We spend a full day carefully selecting from a huge collection of hand-blown, antique glass. We match colors as closely as possible to the color rendering. This is a painstaking task. We hold hundreds of pieces of glass up to different types of lighting to determine how light will affect the finished work. Very powerful light can wash out the colors of a stained glass work and ruin the finished effect. This is to be avoided. Then there is the matter of avoiding colors that clash—and colors that clash under various intensity of light. We select five shades of blue and five shades of yellow. We find the perfect vivid red.

And for the clear glass we want that to be special. We select antique crackle and bubbly, looking at each piece to determine it will have the finished look to match the design.

The most spectacular piece of glass we find is a rose color with swirls of white. This large three-foot by four-foot piece varies in thickness from almost one-half inch to less than one-quarter-inch. When held to the light it has a multitude of rose shading from extremely light to very dark. It is one-of-a-kind. It will make the perfect huge ring that anchors the center of the design.

We load the glass and boxes of lead came into Ken's van and we're on our way to Woodstock.

With the master *cartoon* completed, I begin cutting glass. I am in the studio 16 hours a day, seven days a week for six weeks. My wife drags me out for food.

I've never counted, but I would guess there are close to one-thousand pieces of cut glass in *The Window at St. Catherine's.*

As I make the window I also become aware of remarkable symbolism in the window that to this day I think only Alfred Fisher—who I have never met—and I fully understand.

The matter of shipping the window to England is also on my mind. The window is made in nine sections, three in each light. This makes it possible to place the sections in a crate that will measure only a little over four-feet in height. The crate will be heavy with the antique glass and the lead came.

Bill Cullerton knows John Lunn at British Airways Cargo in Chicago. British Airways agrees to air freight the window from Chicago O'Hare to London's Heathrow at no charge. It will be part of their international cultural exchange program.

John Lunn knows Mark Pflanz, president of Industrial Crating in Elk Grove Village directly adjacent to O'Hare Airport and he agrees to package and crate the window—at no charge.

We load the nine sections of the window in the back of our Volvo and carefully—very carefully—drive to Elk Grove Village. We watch while the sections are packaged and crated.

Next stop London.

◆   ◆   ◆

Good Friday morning Pamela Sharp in Litlington receives a telephone call from a British customs agent at London's Heathrow International. The agent sounds a bit excited. There is a large crate that has just arrived in customs and it is marked *stained glass window, extremely fragile.*

"You need come and pick it up straightaway!" the customs agent said.

Pamela and her husband David drive to Heathrow in a flatbed truck. Within a few hours they return to Litlington with the window. The crate is unloaded with a forklift and rollers are used to move it into St. Catherine's Church.

On Good Friday afternoon the window is on the floor in its crate, delivered to St. Catherine's Church.

With great excitement at the arrival of the window, Pamela, David and Church Warden John Jenner cannot hold back. They open the crate and pull out a section. At a glance they realize this is the genuine article—a true work of stained glass. They are looking at part of *The Window at St. Catherine's.*

PART IV

An Encounter With The Angels

17

Back to The War

Steeple Morden—1945

On leave from *The War* and back in Chicago the week before Christmas 1944 Bill proposes to Elaine "Steve" Stephen. It is something he promised himself he would not do until *The War* is over and he is back home for good. It would be a terrible thing to do to a girl, he thought, to propose to her then leave for *The War* and not return.

Bill has destroyed at least 18 Nazi airplanes and they have not touched him. He is referred to in the Chicago newspapers as a Nazi killer, a destroyer of German air power, a defender of freedom and America. How could you not begin to believe you are invincible. Bill is convinced he is *bulletproof.* Steve is the love of his life and this is the moment to propose. He proposes and Steve accepts.

The Germans surprise the Allies in mid-December 1944 with an enormous winter attack through the Ardennes. Lousy weather keeps American fighters and bombers from providing any assistance in what becomes known as *The Battle of the Bulge.*

Bill receives a telegram asking him to return to Steeple Morden as quickly as possible. As soon as the weather clears over the battlefield, his strafing skills will be in demand.

Bill assures his family and Steve he will soon be back. He returns to *The War.*

◆   ◆   ◆

Steeple Morden Airfield is cold and very damp with intermittent snow and rain upon Bill Cullerton's return. Bill knows it is not as cold on the thermometer as it often is in winters back in Chicago, but somehow it seems colder. The damp cold penetrates to the bones. The new guys—the latest replacement pilots—have taken all the sleeping quarter cots closest to the potbellied stove. His cot is near the drafty doorway.

The good news is that not long after returning, Bill receives a brand new P-51. It is the very latest model, slightly longer, with a little more wing and the clearest canopy.

Bill resumes escorting B-17s and B-24s on bombing runs over Strasbourg, Neuberg, Egmond, Brunswick, Seleststadt, Hamburg, Berlin, Osnabruck and other targets as the United States Army Air Force works to obliterate the Third Reich.

As *The War* goes on the Germans are more and more reluctant to come up to do battle. Weather and flak are the greatest threats to Mustang pilots. In the first two months of 1945, the 355th loses 17 of its Mustangs. Most of them go down after being hit by flak. Others spiral out or simply disappear in the foul winter weather that envelops England. Thick, pea soup fog settles in over the East Anglian plains day-after-day. There are times at the Steeple Morden Airfield that from the cockpit Bill can just make out shadowy figures near the *Miss Steve*. The ground crews lead the Mustangs to the runway for takeoff by having one man stand right next to the fuselage and another 20 feet away near the wing tip. Bill's great hope always is that the pea-soup fog will lift enough by the time he returns so he can see St. Catherine's Church tower and home-in on the runway.

◆   ◆   ◆

One extremely cold and nasty rainy evening Bill Cullerton is enjoying himself in the Crown Pub in Litlington when Father McHugh arrives to see how his boys are behaving. Father McHugh steps up to the bar, stands next to Bill and orders a pint.

"To a short war," Bill toasts Father McHugh.

"Bill I have to ask you. You know you've been attending Mass regularly. I've never seen you take communion," Father McHugh said in his Boston brogue.

"Father, I probably should have told you this a long time ago. I'm not a Catholic," Bill said.

For six months of his first tour, and now a full month into his second tour, Bill has made it appear to Father McHugh that he is a Catholic. He told Father McHugh about his years at Fenwick High School in Oak Park. He probably had bored Father McHugh with his stories of how he played end—at a height of five-foot six-inches—on the Fenwick championship football team. And how he had taken courage from the little sign in Fenwick Coach Tony Lawless' office: *It's not the dog in the fight, but the fight in the dog.* He had told Father McHugh how Coach Lawless influenced his life and instilled in him a passion for striving to be more than he ever thought he could be.

Father McHugh sets his pint back on the bar and steadies himself. He says nothing for what seems to Bill to be several minutes as he digests Bill's news. Here he has asked Bill on several occasions to assist at Mass. He has always thought of Bill as one of his boys, a fellow brought to manhood by the Dominicans at Fenwick High School.

"Well, Bill that is news," Father McHugh said. "Would you like to be a Catholic?"

"Yes, I would," Bill replies.

"Now, Bill, are you certain of that?" Father McHugh asks.

"I have no doubt I would like to be a Catholic," Bill replies.

"Don't leave, I'll be right back," Father McHugh said. He walks over to the bartender and asks to use the telephone.

As far as Bill can see, Father McHugh makes two telephone calls and returns.

"Johnny Ryan is bringing a jeep right over and we'll be on our way to Cambridge in a moment," Father McHugh tells Bill. "We will baptize you tonight. If you're going down, Bill, you're going down a Catholic."

Late at night, in wartime blackout conditions, with small slits cut in the covers over the headlights to provide the bare minimum of light to see where they are going, Father McHugh, Johnny Ryan and Bill are on the road in an Army jeep, on their way to the Catholic Church in Cambridge 15 miles away. They make their way up the winding, narrow country roads. They pass Bassingbourn Airfield. They weave around American servicemen unsteadily pedaling their bicycles from pub-to-pub.

Father McHugh has a friend, a fellow priest in Cambridge. The priest is rousted from his bed to baptize Bill.

There is little ceremony as the Cambridge priest and Father McHugh get right to business. Bill is quickly and officially baptized a Catholic.

Johnny Ryan becomes Bill's godfather.

Father McHugh takes a small gold cross on a chain from his pocket. He places it around Bill's neck and closes the clasp.

"Now if you go down, Bill, you're going down a Catholic," Father McHugh assures him in his Boston brogue.

◆   ◆   ◆

By April 4 there is a touch of spring at the Steeple Morden Airfield. Rain and fog remain a challenge for takeoffs and landings.

This day the 355th Fighter Group is on its way to accompany bombers and then break off to attack German airdromes at Parchim, Perleburg and Kaltenkirchen. Flak in the area is heavy, but routine. Bill sees bursts all around, but as he knows it is the burst you don't see that nails you.

Outside Leipzig Bill and his flight come upon four Focke-Wulf 190Ds. It is a brisk encounter as Bill flies directly above and behind an FW-190 and lets off a short burst of .50-caliber machine gun fire. He can see the bullets striking the body of the plane and bits of what looks like dust are flying off. Bill fires again. The FW-190 rolls over and dives into the ground.

Flying back to the English Channel Bill spots an enormous contrail left in the sky by an extremely fast-moving object. It is a German V-2 rocket en route to London where it will drop out of the sky with no advance warning, explode on impact and wipe out the better part of a city block. There isn't a damn thing Bill and the fighter aircraft can do to stop the V-2s. The only hope is to find them on the ground before they're launched and destroy them.

Upon the return to Steeple Morden Bill radios the others in his flight that he is feeling tired and is going directly in for a landing. There will be no victory rolls or beating up the field this day.

Bill's crew chief Jerry Seidl greets him, noting the covers are off his guns.

"Nailed the SOB," Bill said.

"In the air?" Seidl asks.

"That's right," Bill replies.

"Congratulations, ace," Seidl shakes Bill's hand.

Bill is already an ace four times over when the Nazi planes he has destroyed on the ground are included. But now he is also a legitimate air ace.

"So how's the *Miss Steve?*" Seidl asks.

"Running like a top," Bill replies.

"No problems?" Seidl asks.

"None," Bill said.

Seidl walks around to the front of the *Miss Steve.*

"What in the hell is that?" Seidl said, pointing at a piece of metal sticking in the engine cowling.

"Well, there was some flak," Bill said. But there is always flak. Hardly worth mentioning.

Seidl pulls the engine cover off and peers inside.

"Jeez, look at this," Seidl said. "That piece of metal has gone right into the coolant tank and split the cover. It wouldn't have taken much for that baby to come right off…and then you would have been cooked."

"Good thing we didn't do any victory rolls," Bill said.

"If you had done a victory roll, that cover would have popped off and all your coolant would have drained right out of there and you would have gone in," Seidl said.

And that, Bill believes, is the closest he has come yet to becoming another 355th statistic.

During debriefing the intelligence officers confirm—pending review of the gun film, of course—Bill's destruction of the FW-190. It is Bill Cullerton's fifth confirmed aerial victory, making him an official air ace.

"By the way, Bill, we're still looking over all of your gun footage. We're pretty certain there may be some additional credits coming to you," they tell Bill.

For Bill the *official score* doesn't matter. He wants to kill as many of those Nazi SOBs as he can and get *The War* over with as soon as possible.

18

Explosion & Evasion

Ansbach, Germany—April 8, 1945

At 11:25 in the morning, the 357th Fighter Squadron makes rendezvous with a flight of B-24 bombers over Dornstadt, Germany. At 12:20 p.m. the bombs fall on Roth Airdrome and at 12:40 the 357th finishes its escort mission and sweeps south to the Oberphaffenhofen and Augsburg area.

Bill Cullerton takes his flight down to strafe the Ansbach Airdrome. Bill starts his group at 15,000 feet, dives toward the ground, leveling off to fly toward the airdrome at treetop level. As Bill leads his flight across the airdrome he tilts the nose of *Miss Steve* down slightly and begins firing. He swings up, gains altitude and brings his flight around from east-to-west.

As Bill approaches the airdrome he feels the blow. It is as if someone has thrown a one-ton boulder at the *Miss Steve*. She shudders. Bill knows at once the *Miss Steve* has been hit by flak. The damn flak gunners have nailed him. He pulls back the stick and gives the *Miss Steve* all the throttle he can to gain altitude. He smells smoke. He looks in the mirror. Flames are leaping up right behind the cockpit. The *Miss Steve* has been hit in the fuselage fuel tank directly behind the cockpit. The 100-octane fuel is burning hot right behind him.

All of Bill's training tells him to roll the *Miss Steve* over and fall out of the Mustang. That—by the book—is the only way to successfully bail from a P-51. There's no time for the book now.

Bill jettisons the canopy. The *Miss Steve* pitches forward and shoots him out like a rock from a slingshot. As he rolls in the air Bill sees his pack of Lucky Strikes fly over his head. He makes a grab for them and misses. He begins tumbling rapidly. He feels as if he's still going 300 miles an hour except without the protection of *Miss Steve's* cockpit. He is a missile. He knows he's hurtling through the air but it seems as if everything is moving in slow motion. He pulls the parachute ripcord…and *bang!* The parachute opens and he takes a tremendous jolt. It feels like the parachute straps around his torso have been pulled into his chest and shoulders. His forward motion slams to a halt. Seconds after he feels the jolt, his backside hits the ground hard.

The wallop he takes knocks the wind out of him. He sees the *Miss Steve* still going forward in a massive ball of bright orange, yellow and red. When 100-octane fuel burns, it burns hot. Bill hears the impact and explosion. He believes the *Miss Steve* has blown-up at least a quarter-mile beyond where he is sitting on the ground, trying to breathe.

Harsh reality overcomes Bill. He has been shot down. He is on the ground. He is behind enemy lines He is not far from a German airdrome—an airdrome he has been shooting up trying to kill the bastards.

All of the training leaps to his mind. *Evade.* The mission now is to *evade.* Make those damn Nazis use up all their manpower to try and find you. *Evade.*

Bill leaps to his feet and begins running as fast as he can. He's never run so hard in his life. He is running full force and not making any forward progress. It's as if he is running in heavy sand on a beach along Lake Michigan. He is running and running and going nowhere. It's like a nightmare. Then he realizes he has not unhitched his parachute harness. He is running trying to pull his parachute.

As Bill unhitches the parachute harness he talks to himself: "Calm down! Calm down!"

There are no Nazis shooting at him—at least not yet. He bailed out so close to the ground they might not even have seen him. Bill pulls the parachute into a pile and leaves it at the side of an open field. He takes off at a run for a pine forest about 100 yards off to his right. He finds an enormous pine tree with limbs right down to the ground and he crawls under the tree. He wraps his body around the tree trunk and catches his breath.

Bill hears sirens. For some odd reason the sirens make Bill relax. And in relaxing he begins to think more clearly. He hopes that placing the parachute on the other side of the open field will throw the Germans off his trail. Running further in an attempt to escape seems like a bad idea. There are damn Nazis all over the place. They have vehicles. They have dogs. They have machine guns. Concealment under the massive bows of the huge pine tree until it is dark seems the best approach.

Bill pulls out his .45-caliber pistol. He's not certain what one .45 can possibly do in this situation, but it somehow makes him feel better.

Within minutes of crawling under the pine tree, Bill hears the German soldiers calling to one another as they spread out around the open field. He hears them shout. One of them must have found his parachute. Now they know he did not burn up with the *Miss Steve.* They know he is on the ground. And in the short time from the *Miss Steve* exploding until now they also know he cannot have gone far.

Bill hugs his body around the tree trunk. He still has the .45 pistol in his hands. Then he sees four boots right at the edge of the tree limbs and he hears two German soldiers talking. They aren't moving. Bill could reach out and touch their boots, they are that close to him. He sees their gun butts on the ground. Bill smells cigarette smoke. Hell, these guys are screwing off. They aren't looking for him. Bill thinks that if they took a leak they would find him and he would give up. After what must be a half-hour, they flick off their cigarettes, pick up their guns and walk off.

Bill begins to relax and wait for dark.

◆   ◆   ◆

The intelligence officers at Steeple Morden Airfield give a shot glass full of brandy to Bob Garlich. From his P-51, the *Luscious Lu,* he tells the intelligence guys he saw the *Miss Steve* go down in a ball of fire. Garlich did not see a parachute. He reports they were all right down on-the-deck shooting up the airdrome. The *Miss Steve* was right down there with them, not more than 100 feet above ground—maybe lower. The *Miss Steve* was a burning wreck when he last saw her and Cullerton has to be gone right along with her, Garlich reports.

Taking into consideration what they hear from Garlich, but with no absolute positive information that he is dead, the intelligence officers at Steeple Morden Airfield report Bill Cullerton missing-in-action.

◆   ◆   ◆

One of the buttons on Bill's flight suit has a finely machined screw cap. He loosens the cap and now has a compass in his hands. He knows he wants to go west—west toward the Allied lines. Still under the pine bows it is difficult to see the compass needle. It appears to him that west is directly through the airdrome. He will have to work his way around the airdrome in order to go west.

Bill checks his watch. It's 1800 hours—6:00 p.m. In the pine forest darkness is arriving faster than in the open field to the west—toward the airdrome. He waits another hour.

Carefully, slowly Bill crawls out from under the pine tree. He rises to a crouch and looks in all directions. He sees no one—no Germans, no vehicles, nothing. He heads north planning to work his way on a very long circle around the airfield which he reasons will be well guarded and patrolled.

In the twilight Bill notices the woods are immaculately clean. There are no tree branches on the ground, no shrubs or vines of any kind. It's like taking a walk through Chicago's Columbus Park. The trees are beautiful, perfect fir trees. However, the woods are also very disorienting.

As the last sunlight disappears it is absolutely pitch black. The big fir trees choke out the light. Bill can't see the sky, so there isn't even starlight. All of Germany is in total blackout at night. There are no lights coming from any buildings or yards. It is as if you went in a room at night with no windows and closed the door. He feels as if someone has put blindfolds on his eyes.

Bill pulls a waterproof matchbox from a pocket in his flight suit. The matchbox is not standard issue. It is something Bill remembered from his scouting days. He made it himself. It is waterproof and contains stove matches. He lights a match so he can see the compass. Damn, he's heading east—wrong direction! Hell, if he keeps going that way he'll end up in

Russia. He swings to the west. After another half hour of walking through the pine forest, Bill lights another match and checks the compass. Still heading west. Wait a minute! The compass is luminous. There's no need for matches. The needle pointer and directions are all luminous.

Bill sits down for a moment. He has to calm down. He has to think rationally. So far, so good. The Nazi bastards have not found him and they do not seem to be on his trail—at least not yet. This is all good news. He must remain calm. He takes several deep breaths, stands up and starts walking. In the pitch black he walks right into a tree. This is not going to be easy.

◆　　　◆　　　◆

Many veteran pilots of the 355th Fighter Group gather in the Officer's Club at Steeple Morden. It is a wake for Bill Cullerton—their comrade "Cully."

Over the first drink they each confirm it to all present to be certain that somehow one of them had seen it and no one else had—there was no parachute. How could there have been a parachute? The *Miss Steve* was on-the-deck. They all know you need at least 1,000 feet of altitude for the chute to open and let you drift to the ground. Cully was not more than 100 feet off-the-deck—probably lower than that—when the *Miss Steve* took the hit. Of that they are all certain. And they know you don't parachute to the ground from 100 feet.

No one says it, but the veterans know. Here was a *bulletproof* pilot if ever one existed. And he is gone, just like that.

They can all still see it. They replay it in their minds over and over again. First the *Miss Steve* is a blowtorch streaming blazing hot flames. She seems to nose up momentarily and then pitches down. As she roars toward the ground, a great ball of fire envelops her. And they know it is almost for certain Cully—their comrade, the *bulletproof* fighter pilot—is consumed in the yellow, orange and red fiery ball stoked by 100-octane fuel.

They also know that tomorrow morning they will each climb back in the cockpits of their P-51s and go back to *The War*.

◆   ◆   ◆

At daybreak, Bill Cullerton finds a wooded area and walks a good distance back among the trees. He finds a couple of smaller fir trees and settles in their bows. He feels as if he is a hunted animal. He knows it's not a good idea to move in the open during the day. He would be spotted by the Germans for certain. He will rest during the day and travel at night. But God he is hungry.

Bill watches as a crew of farm workers moves down a road just the other side from the forest. Bill suspects they are slave laborers. They're hand-planting potatoes. He will wait until dark and dig up some of those seed potatoes.

As the sun sets, Bill moves into the potato field and begins digging with his hands to try to find the seed potatoes. The ground is very hard and already frosted. His hands begin bleeding and he is finding no potatoes. He gives this up as a bad idea. But he is so hungry.

Bill begins walking through the woods. He comes upon a trail and decides to stay on that for a while. He checks his compass and he's going west—the right direction to move toward Allied lines.

In the dark Bill hears a noise, which seems not far away. He stops and listens. He hears it again. It is a door opening and closing. He must be near a house or a barn or buildings of some kind. In the blackness surrounding him he can't see any buildings. He hunches down and moves toward the sound. Then he sees a little sliver of light coming through a slit in a curtain. It is a house. He knows there are people in there. He decides to look for their garbage can. They must have a garbage can. There would be food in the garbage can. Bill circles the house and looks around the buildings nearby. No garbage can. No food of any kind. He makes his way back to the path and keeps moving west.

Suddenly lights are flashing in the forest directly ahead. Bill drops to the ground. He raises his head and the lights are still flashing. First they flash to his right. Then they flash to his left. The damn Germans are out here with flashlights trying to find him. How many are there? Do they have dogs? Did someone see him back at that house and report him to the Gestapo? Have they already spotted him on the trail and they're preparing to hose the area with machine gun fire?

Bill hugs the ground and doesn't move for several minutes. He slowly raises his head. He can feel his heart thumping. The lights on his right are still flashing, but the light is a very odd color. It is greenish and doesn't flash so much as it pulses.

Nothing seems to be moving in the forest. There are no human sounds, no clicking sounds of anyone preparing to fire weapons.

Then Bill remembers where he has seen that light before. During the summers of his high school years he was a guide in northern Wisconsin. It has to be phosphorescent light emitting from rotting trees. Under normal conditions you can seldom see this light because it is faint. But in the darkness of a moonless night in northern Wisconsin, and here in the heavy fir forests of Germany it is so dark that the phosphorescent light pulses.

Bill rises up on his elbows and studies the light to be certain that's what he's seeing. No question. Phosphorescent light from rotting fir trees.

Bill stands up and keeps moving. He checks his compass—still going west.

It is daylight all too soon. Bill finds another clump of smaller fir trees and stays in them resting again until dark.

◆   ◆   ◆

Steeple Morden Airfield has heard nothing more about the probable loss of Lieutenant Bill Cullerton in a fiery, most likely fatal crash of the *Miss Steve.*

In the crew quarters that are home to the pilots, the veterans open Cully's trunk. It is the unwritten rule that when one of their comrades is lost in *The War* his belongings go to those who survive. Personal effects such as the missing comrade's best uniform, pictures of his parents and girlfriend, personal letters are packaged and sent to his parents back in the States. Everything else is fair game.

Sergeant Booth packages Bill's personal effects and best uniform and sees that they are on their way to Bill's parents in Chicago.

The veteran pilots divvy up everything that remains.

◆   ◆   ◆

It is dark and Bill is on the move—heading west. He stays on the trail he found. It is easy going and seems to wind through the forest. He cannot tell if it is an old game trail worn down by deer or small animals or if it is a hiking trail.

Bill is moving along as well as he can in the pitch-black fir forest. The trees here have to be over 100-feet tall and form a canopy that blocks out all light. He stays on the path and is making no noise. There is an explosion of large animal noise directly in front of him. He is so close to whatever it is that the animal brushes Bill as it leaps to escape. Bill jumps back. He starts running. His heart is racing as he runs through the woods. He can hear the animal crashing through tree limbs. A large pine bow snaps and slaps Bill in the face. He stops running. It had to have been a deer lying in the path hoping like hell Bill would stop coming toward it. When Bill kept coming, the deer was left with no choice but to leap up and run for its life. Bill shared the feeling. If only he had known the damn deer was there. He would have taken his knife and killed it on the spot and eaten parts of it raw.

Then he remembers the chocolate bar! Of course. How could he have forgotten? In one pocket of his flight suit is a chocolate bar, packed there just in the event a pilot is down and evading. Bill pats around on his flight suit, looking for the pocket with the chocolate bar. There it is! He eats the whole thing.

Bill pulls himself together and starts back down the path. He does not go far before he comes to a stream. It appears in the dark to be a fairly wide stream. Looking for a place to cross, Bill makes his way to his right. There is no bridge, no log across, no easy way over. He goes to his left with the same results. Thinking he might be able to jump the stream, he starts looking for a place it narrows. In the dark his depth perception has gone to hell. But there are not many choices. Bill backs up on a clear, flat spot and takes a running leap. He lands right in the middle of the stream. He is soaked to the skin with ice-cold water. Bill wrings his clothes out as best he can and waits for daylight. He is so cold he begins shaking and cannot stop shaking.

At daylight Bill knows he will have to find sunlight to dry out and he will have to keep moving in an attempt to warm his body.

As he keeps walking he realizes he is in a valley and the damn stream keeps wandering around and appearing in front of him. Bill knows he cannot go in that damn stream again. He will freeze to death if he does.

Warm sunlight begins drying Bill's clothes and he is about three-quarters dry when he sees a bridge in a very small village. He sees two German soldiers leaning against a building by the bridge talking to some girls. Bill makes his way to the edge of the village and finds a bicycle. He hops on and rides the bicycle across the bridge, right past the two German soldiers and the girls. They holler something at Bill. He doesn't understand a word of German and calls back—"Yah, Yah." They all laugh and Bill keeps pedaling. Bill imagines they think he is a German flyer. Who knows what an American or German flight suit looks like? If you're a German grunt standing on a small bridge talking with a couple of pretty young girls the fact some guy in a flight suit goes by on a bicycle is of little concern. Who cares? And who knows what they said to him? Maybe something like: "Hey, flyboy, where's your airplane?" Whatever they said, Bill's "Yah, yah" response gave them all a laugh.

What the German soldiers don't know is Bill is carrying his .45 pistol under his arm, under his flight suit.

Bill pedals a couple of miles beyond the village and believes he has now successfully made his way past the damn stream. He's almost completely dry. He ditches the bicycle beside the road and heads back into the forest to wait for nightfall.

◆   ◆   ◆

Official notification of next-of-kin is a relatively slow-moving process as *The War* proceeds at a ferocious cost of American lives. It is becoming apparent to the officials at Steeple Morden Airfield that Bill Cullerton is at best missing-in-action…and very probably killed-in-action.

It is time to put the wheels in motion to notify Bill's parents back in Chicago. It is time to report Bill missing-in-action—to let the next-of-kin down slowly—to prepare them for the worst. By April 1945 there is a blizzard of notifications moving through the official channels in an attempt to keep those back on the home front informed about the condition of their loved ones. Because of the volume of notifications the paperwork moves slowly.

◆   ◆   ◆

He doesn't wait for full darkness, but starts off just as the sun is setting. Bill Cullerton is emboldened by the bike ride over the bridge and through the village. He finds another trail through the pine forest. It is leading in the right direction—west—so he stays on the trail.

Then he hears the sound of a barking dog not too far away. The dog is howling and baying the way Bill has heard dogs on-the-hunt do. Now the damn Nazis have turned the dogs loose to find him. The barking and howling is coming closer. He can't tell if there is one dog or a bunch of dogs. The howling grows louder.

Bill pulls out his .45 pistol and sits down in the middle of the trail. It is still twilight so there is some light in the woods. He remembers taking hunting dogs into the field to flush birds. The dogs would always howl and bark until they were within 150 feet or so of the birds. Then the dogs would fall silent and bear down on their target. Bill reasons that when the dogs fall silent they will be within a few yards of him. He sits in the middle of the trail, knowing the dogs will come right at him. The howling and barking stops. Bill can hear the dog's paws slap on the hard trail surface.

Then he hears the snorts as the dog lunges forward. In the air, right there in front of him, is the dog he has been expecting. It is in an extended leap, jaws open, ready to pounce on him. Bill aims and pulls the trigger. The blast from Bill's .45 takes the dog further up in the air, stops its forward movement and drops it on the trail not more than five feet from Bill. He takes a quick look at the monster dog. It is a schnauzer with an enormous head and must weigh 150 pounds.

Bill leaps to his feet and sprints away from the area. If the damn Nazis had turned the dog loose to find him, they certainly heard the shot from Bill's .45. He runs and keeps running through the fir trees, knocking off branches, bouncing off trees and stumbling over logs for at least 20 minutes. Then he stops. He listens. There are no sounds in the woods. Silence.

Bill is disoriented. He pulls out the compass and takes a heading due west. He has lost the trail and is now making his way through the pitch-black forest. He can only make out shadows in front of him as he walks. He feels as if he is a blind man as he bumps into tree trunks he can't see and trips over logs on the ground. He keeps moving until he begins to see daylight. Just ahead he sees an opening, a large meadow, and just across the meadow is a farm field. Figures are moving in the field. Bill stops and crouches trying to see if they are German soldiers once again out looking for him.

As the sun rises Bill can see a German soldier carrying a rifle strapped to his shoulder. The figures are farm workers, probably slave laborers working under the watch of the German solider. They are planting something by hand—probably potatoes. God a raw potato would taste so good right now. Any kind of food would taste good.

Bill watches as the workers move up and down the field, crouched over, planting. He sees that a young girl working in the field is moving away from the group and coming in his direction as she plants. She is dressed in what Bill believes are peasant clothes, nothing very fancy. She moves closer and closer to the tree line that hides Bill from view. The nearest field worker to her is now at least a quarter-mile distant. The German solider is a great distance away and appears to be smoking a cigarette. Bill decides to take a chance. He pulls out his pistol and emerges from the woods. He quickly approaches the girl and let's her see he is holding a gun.

The girl realizes immediately that Bill is an escapee.

"Amerikanski?" she asks.

Bill had heard the Russians call him by the same name.

"Yes, American," Bill responds. He can't tell if she is Polish, or Czech or Russian. Using sign language he indicates he is hungry.

She holds up her hand and extends her index finger, turns and walks away. A few minutes later she is back with raw potatoes, some black bread, and water. The bread is pitted with small maggots. Bill consumes all of the food and it is delicious—maggots and all.

Amused, the girl watches Bill eat. When he is done, Bill indicates with hand signals that he would have to be on his way.

She points at herself, then at Bill, and then off in the distance. She wants to go with him.

Bill is having enough trouble moving on his own without having a young girl along. He also realizes that if they are caught—the two of them together—the young girl is a goner. The Nazis will shoot her on the spot. She is a classic babushka-wearing Eastern European slave laborer. The Nazis will kill her if they catch her escaping and assisting an American pilot evading capture.

Bill shakes his head. The girl begins crying. Bill turns and moves on. He is still heading west, putting some distance between himself and the young girl and anyone who might have seen them. After about one hour of walking in the pine forest, Bill stops and waits for darkness.

As the sun is setting, Bill hears *karuuump*. Then another. It sounds a little like rolling thunder. It is artillery fire. It must be quite a distance from him, but there is no question he is hearing artillery fire. He checks his compass and keeps heading west. He must be moving close to the front lines.

Bill begins thinking as he is walking in the pitch dark that moving through the Germans and finding the Americans as they're shooting at each other could be a tricky proposition. There is not much point in worrying about it. Somehow this will all work out and he will be back at Steeple Morden Airfield soon.

Light begins breaking through the huge fir trees. Bill hears louder artillery fire. In addition to the *karuuump,* he now hears a sharper sound and it seems closer to him. He thinks he is hearing the American artillery in the distance, and then the German 88s responding. All of the artillery sounds are much closer.

Bill stops in the woods. The fir trees here are at least 100 feet tall. The forest floor is completely barren of any tree limbs or underbrush. It looks to Bill as if you could spread out a blanket and have a picnic any place. It is a perfect park.

Whooosh...Kaboom. Whooosh...Kaboom. Artillery shells are hitting the treetops right over Bill. Parts of shredded pine trees are flying in every direction. Great clusters of huge fir treetops are cascading down in thunderous, roaring avalanches. Bill sees an enormous chunk of a fir tree blasted away and shot through the trunk of another tree. Shell after shell hits the treetops directly over Bill. He dives for the ground. There are great cracking, splintering, roaring sounds as treetops topple 100 feet to the ground crashing down near him.

Bill knows these are American shells. The American artillery is blanketing the German lines and covering the infantry advance and he is caught in the shelling.

This is no place to be. Bill knows he needs to get out of the woods in a hurry. He begins running and the shells keep bursting overhead, blasting away at the treetops with pieces of fir shrapnel flying in every direction. As he nears the forest edge, he sees an open meadow and another pine forest just on the other side. There is no choice. In open daylight he makes a run for it across the open meadow. He sprints over a small knoll and there—right in front of him not more than 20 feet away—stand a dozen Waffen-SS Nazis. They are all black-suited with the lightning strike on their collars. He is eyeball-to-eyeball with the worst bastards in the German army—Waffen-SS. A dozen guns are aimed directly at Bill. There is nothing to do but raise his arms and surrender.

The Germans are obviously retreating. They are pulling back as the American artillery zeros in on them. They were standing in the meadow for a smoke when Bill came over the knoll and ran straight into them.

Hat slightly askew, the thin, gray-eyed Waffen-SS officer walks directly up to Bill.

"Pistol," he motions to Bill.

Bill has no choice but to hand over his .45. Ten other Waffen-SS have their guns aimed directly at him.

The Waffen-SS officer takes Bill's gun, jams it against his right side just under his rib cage.

"For you the war is over," the Waffen-SS officer says. He pulls the trigger.

Bill never hears the shot. He sees his right arm swing up as his body is spun in the air and he slams over backward and hits the ground, falling on his back.

◆   ◆   ◆

Bright sunlight streams on Bill Cullerton's face as he lies face-up in the German meadow. He comes to slowly, painfully. God he hurts.

Bill moves his arms and then his legs. He feels he is soaking wet. Then he remembers what happened and realizes he has been shot. Where? Where was he shot? He recalls the Waffen-SS bastard taking his .45 and shoving it up against him. He remembers nothing after that.

He reaches with his left hand and feels just under his right rib cage where the Waffen-SS bastard had held the .45. Bill can feel it is very wet. He wipes his hand over the spot and raises it up to look at it. His hand is bright red with blood.

He stretches his left hand around behind his back. He is afraid of what he will feel there. Bill has seen deer hit with a gunshot. The bullet expands as it goes through the flesh. There might be a small hole on the entry site, but a huge crater on the exit side. He carefully reaches around to his back expecting to be able to put his fist in the opening. He can feel only a small hole. The area around the hole is soaking wet. He holds his hand up again and sees it is bright red. But there is no large bullet exit of torn flesh that he can feel.

Bill passes out.

◆   ◆   ◆

In Oak Park Illinois Elaine "Steve" Stephen is busy planning her wedding to her high school sweetheart and now fiancé Bill Cullerton. Steve reserves Oak Park's Ascension Church for the Saturday, June 30, 1945 wedding ceremony. She selects six attendants including three junior bridesmaids.

Steve's father is not at all happy about the wedding planning she is doing. He, of course, knows Steve's fiancé is a *War Hero*. But the fact is he could be killed. He might not come home. And his daughter is planning a wedding.

Steve tells her father she knows Bill is a very tough fellow, a durable guy and that he will not die in *The War,* he will come home and they will be married. It is time to plan the wedding!

Steve's father cannot dissuade her. How will he possibly console her if the young man fails to return?

Her mother decides it would be a good idea to call the groom's parents and let them know the wedding date has been finalized.

Steve is a determined bride and the June 30 wedding planning continues. There is much to be done!

◆   ◆   ◆

Bill shivers as he comes to. He tries to open his eyes. They seem to be frozen shut. Slowly he is able to open them ever so slightly. Through the narrow slits he sees what appear to be crystals. His eyelids have frosted shut during the night.

Slowly the sunlight warms his face, and the frost on his eyelids thaws. He is shivering.

What has happened? Where is he? Then he again remembers the Waffen-SS bastard sticking his .45 up against him.

With his left hand Bill reaches again for the spot the bullet entered his body. He touches the area. It is no longer wet, the blood has dried. He slowly works his hand around behind his back. Again, there is no wetness. The pain is horrendous.

Bill lies as still as he can thinking that if he moves he will start bleeding again.

White, puffy clouds stream over in the bright blue April sky.

And that's when he sees them.

They are as real as could be up in the sky, emerging from around the clouds. There are three of them. Three angels are coming down toward him. They are coming to take him. He knows that is the reason they are here. The angels are as real as anything he has ever seen. They are coming down from the puffy white clouds. This is it. He is going to die. The angels are coming to take him.

Bill feels something lift his right hand. Is this how the angels will take him…simply lift him by his right hand and float him skyward?

Bill looks to his right. There is a man hunched over pulling his watch off his wrist. It's a damn German body looter. Bill groans. The figure jumps back. Whoever it is did not think Bill is alive and they are startled when he groans.

Bill feels himself being lifted up and dragged. He then sees a two-wheel horse cart. He is dumped on the cart. The pain is excruciating. He can feel he is wet again where the Waffen-SS bastard shot him. He is bleeding again. The cart rumbles off and Bill passes out.

When he comes to he is stretched out on a table. Someone is looking down at him. They are lifting his chain and cross in their hand. They are saying something to him.

"Cat-o-leek? Cat-o-leek?"

Through his fog he begins to understand someone is asking him if he is a Catholic. Best to tell the truth. The angels might have lifted him to heaven for all he knows.

"Yes," Bill mumbles. "Where am I?"

"In a hospital in Feuchtwangen, Germany. I am a doctor," the person tells Bill in very broken English. "There are no priests here. You have been shot through the liver."

The doctor leans over Bill and whispers in his ear:

"I am a Jew. I will help you. My name is Meier."

The doctor resumes talking in a normal voice.

"You've been shot through the liver. You are bleeding internally and there is nothing we can do. You are going to bleed to death," the doctor said. "Do you want to write a note to your parents? I will see they receive it."

"No," Bill said. He is very discouraged at being told he is bleeding to death. He does not trust the doctor. He doesn't trust anybody. But somehow Dr. Meier impresses him. Bill knows Dr. Meier is on his side or he would not have taken the time to examine him and talk with him.

"Do you have any sulfa drugs?" Bill asks.

"No," Dr. Meier said.

Bill could tell by the look on the doctor's face he had no idea what Bill was talking about. Sulfa drugs, what are they?

Bill passes out.

◆　　　◆　　　◆

When Bill comes to he is in a hospital bed in a ward filled with wounded German soldiers. He can see newspapers wrapped around the feet of many of them. And around the hands of others. He studies them for a while, and then it occurs to him the Germans have run out of bandages. They are using newspapers for bandages. He wonders why all the hands and feet are wrapped and then it hits him. These are German soldiers defeated in the 900-day battle of Leningrad, Russia. They have walked all the way back to Germany with frostbitten hands and feet.

One of the German soldiers starts to speak to Bill in German. Bill shakes his head. Several of the wounded Germans look at him, and they realize he is an American. They start a furious protest. Dr. Meier is called and the German soldiers point at Bill from their beds. They want this American out of *their* ward.

Dr. Meier moves Bill to a private room. And there Bill's caretakers begin arriving. In addition to Dr. Meier there are three others in the hospital willing to risk their lives for Bill.

First is a very young—maybe 14-year-old—Dutch boy who appears to speak no English and Bill thinks is probably a slave laborer.

Bill spends most of his day lying on his back as still as he can hoping that whatever wounds were caused when the .45 slug passed through his body might heal. There is nothing else to do. He sleeps as much as possible and moves as little as he has to.

The Dutch boy arrives every now and then by his bed. He's carrying bedpans, carrying water and constantly mopping the floors. Every once in a while he secretly slips Bill a piece of bread.

The nurses are German Lutheran nuns. Bill learns they came from a cloister somewhere up in the Bavarian Alps. Bill guesses the nuns—who dressed in habits—have no nursing training other than what they received from Dr. Meier on the job. Probably some Gestapo type arrived at their cloister one day and ordered them to become nurses in Feuchtwangen. So here they are. The nuns like Bill. Two of them arrive at his bedside a couple of times a day. One reads from the Bible in German while the other lifts up her habit and pulls potatoes from her undergarments and secretly hands them to Bill.

At great personal risk the little Dutch boy and the German Lutheran nuns sneak food to Bill. They keep him alive.

"The Germans have received a report you are here," Dr. Meier tells Bill. "They want to take you. But I have told them if they take you they must sign for you. I have told them if they take you and move you, it will kill you. I have told them I want someone from the military to sign for you because when the Americans come I do not want to be the fellow they are looking for. They will not sign, so you stay."

A few days later two German soldiers appear in Bill's room. They drag Bill from his bed and take him out in the hallway near the top of a stairwell. They drop him down the stairs.

Dr. Meier hears the ruckus.

In great pain, Bill watches the hand gestures to try to follow the shouting match that ensues between Dr. Meier and the German soldiers.

"Oh, he just fell down the stairs," one of the German soldiers tells Dr. Meier with a shrug.

Dr. Meier knows they pushed Bill down the stairs. He is irate.

"Leave. If you will not sign for him, leave him," Dr. Meier said, pointing toward the exit.

The German soldiers leave.

Dr. Meier and the Dutch boy help Bill back to the bed.

Although Bill cannot see the blood, he knows he is bleeding again. He feels the wetness. And he hurts. He really hurts. It is a searing pain flashing through his right side.

Dr. Meier stays with Bill for a while.

"I am the only doctor in this hospital. I am the only doctor in Feuchtwangen. There are 6,000 people in this area and I am the only doctor," Dr. Meier talks as he examines Bill's wounds.

"All of the doctors and nurses from here were sent to German military hospitals. The Nazis shipped me here from Munich. They knew I was a doctor and they needed a doctor. So that just leaves me and the nuns," Dr. Meier said.

◆   ◆   ◆

A few days later Bill finds out the Dutch boy knows a little English.

"Be careful janitor," the Dutch boy whispers to Bill as he slips him some bread "He's Nazi. He tell soldiers in town everything happen here. He's Nazi. He's bad."

Bill continues to rest. The bleeding stops and he feels less pain each day. The nuns appear twice daily with their Bible reading and slip him potatoes from under their habits.

Bill begins to think he might not die.

◆   ◆   ◆

Dr. Meier comes in Bill's room and closes the door. He comes close to Bill and begins speaking very quietly.

"You must leave. The Germans are pulling back. They keep coming here for you. I keep telling them they must sign if they take you. They won't sign. But tomorrow they say they are taking you with them, you are a prisoner and they are taking you with them as they pull back. They are coming tomorrow morning for you. If they take you, you will die. I have had a load of manure put under your window. You will go out the window. Then you must go as far from here as you can," Dr. Meier said. He turns and leaves the room.

The young Dutch boy brings Bill a pillow. Bill looks inside. It is his flight suit, the clothes he had been wearing when he was brought to the hospital. He looks for his watch and then he remembers the body looter who was taking it off his wrist when he was lying in the field. There is no watch. The SOB must have taken it.

Bill has had time to think about the damn German body looter. That had to be what he was doing out in the field looking for watches, rings, pistols and whatever else he could find. Bill believes the only reason the body looter loaded him on the cart and brought him to the hospital in Feuchtwangen is he thought Bill was a German pilot. Who knew the difference between a German flight suit and an American flight suit? Maybe if the body looter brought in a wounded German pilot he would receive a reward. Bill does not believe it was through any generous act of kindness to a wounded American that the body looter delivered him to the hospital. The SOB was looking for a payoff in addition to the loot he was collecting off of bodies in the fields.

As soon as it is dark Bill pulls himself out of bed and locks his door. He puts on the flight suit. He feels something hard in the right-hand pocket. He reaches in and pulls out his military identity card. It is called an *AGO* card or *Adjutant General Officer's* card. The card has his picture, name, rank and serial number. There is a hole in the middle of it where the .45

slug passed through. He opens the window and looks down. In the evening light he sees the pile of manure directly under the window. But suddenly it does not look to him as if he is on the second floor, it looks more as if he is on the sixth floor. It looks like the manure pile is 100 feet below his window. He is afraid he is going to knock himself out when he hits the pile. He moves out on the window ledge and sits there. He tries to recall how the parachute guys jump. He seems to remember that when they're practicing they jump off a 20-foot stand and roll over and have no trouble. He is in no shape to do any rolling. He decides the best thing to do is to land feetfirst, right in the shit. He sits a while longer. Then he decides the sooner he gets going, the sooner he can recover if he hurts himself in the fall. Hell, he does not have a choice. It is either jump and escape or be taken by the damn Nazis who will kill him. His heart is beating faster as he pushes himself away from the window ledge and jumps feetfirst.

Bill lands softly but with a huge squish. Shit flies all over the place. Jeez it smells horrible. It must be pig shit...ripe, rotten pig shit. The sour stench almost makes him vomit. He works his way out of the manure pile and moves across the yard.

Which way to go? Which way is Feuchtwangen? He believes he will be better off moving away from the town. But which way is the town? He goes down hill and walks along a field beside a road. The fall from the window has opened his wounds and he is bleeding again. He cannot go far. He sees a big culvert under the roadway and he crawls in. It is bitterly cold. He stinks of pig shit, he is bleeding and he is exhausted. He falls asleep.

◆   ◆   ◆

Bill is awakened by the high-pitched roar of a tank. It passes directly over him. The roar inside the culvert is deafening. He is fairly certain it is a German tank. He has heard the German engines before and they have a high-pitched whining sound. The damn Germans always seem to have their motors revved up, and they whine.

Bill runs his hand over the pocket of his flight suit. It is dry so he is not bleeding.

There is the whining roar of another tank. Then another and another. Dozens of tanks pass directly over Bill. He hears what must be motorcycles. There are a lot of motorcycles; there must be hundreds of them. Then he hears more tanks followed by horse carts. It takes hours for all of the traffic to pass over the culvert.

Then there is silence. Absolute, total silence.

Bill stays in the culvert. He does not dare peak out. Several hours pass. Nothing crosses on the road above the culvert. He feels he must be in no-man's-land, the area between heavily armed combatants where no animal or person would ever want to be.

It is once again dark and Bill falls asleep curled up in the culvert.

He awakens and can't open his eyes. He rubs his eyes and wipes ice crystals from them. Frost has formed on his eyelids during the night. He is so cold and hungry.

Bill hears the faint sound of a low rumble, barely audible in the culvert. It slowly grows in intensity until it is directly above him. This must be the rumble of the American tanks. Bill waits for the first one to pass over. There is a deafening roar inside the culvert. He decides it is time to crawl out and see what is happening along the road above him.

There they are—a huge number of American tanks rumbling along the road on their way to Feuchtwangen.

A gunner on top of one of the tanks—a very big black-American—spots Bill and swings the biggest machine gun Bill has ever seen directly at him. Bill throws his hands in the air: "American pilot. American pilot."

Even in his confused state, Bill realizes the gunner has every reason to pull the trigger. Who the hell is this guy saying he is an American pilot in the middle of this Nazi-infested countryside. He could just as easily be one of the fanatics ready to pitch a grenade. Their country is crumbling around them and the damn Nazi fanatics are still killing Americans.

"I don't care what you are. Don't move!" the tank gunner shouts at Bill.

A half-dozen U.S. infantrymen run down the embankment toward Bill, their rifles aimed right at him.

"Who the hell are you?" one of them asks.

"American pilot. 355th Fighter Group, Steeple Morden," Bill responds, hands in the air.

"Who does Ted Williams play for?" they ask Bill.

"Boston Red Sox," Bill said.

And at that, they stop aiming their rifles at him, the tank gunner moves his machine gun in a different direction, and all of the Americans start cheering.

"We've got an American pilot! We've got an American pilot!" they shout.

More shouting breaks out along the road as news travels back through the spearhead group of the United States Army 12th Armored Division. They are probing to see what lies ahead of the main advance. And they have recovered an American pilot!

Bill is exhausted and sits down.

"Are you wounded?" an infantryman asks.

"Shot through the stomach," Bill replies. "But I'm better than I was."

"Hey, he's wounded!" the infantryman shouts up to others on the road. "Bring some blankets! Start a fire—we need to warm this guy up."

Ten blankets appear and Bill is stretched out on them and they start a small fire.

"Hey, who's got the brandy?" another infantryman shouts. A bottle of liberated brandy appears, its contents poured into a canteen, and offered to Bill. It tastes fantastic. Bill takes two or three major swigs...then sips some more. Bill thinks the GI answer to saving a guy's life is to give him some brandy. Bill decides it is pretty good stuff. He keeps sipping.

"This guy is hungry! Boil up some eggs!" another tanker said. And they boil some eggs they've liberated along the way. Bill enjoys about four farm-fresh, boiled eggs. Then the eggs hit the brandy. Bill throws up.

The tank commanders appear to Bill to be having a major consultation. They are all thrilled they've saved an American pilot, but now they have an additional challenge. How to get Bill back to a field hospital. One of them comes down and talks with Bill.

"Look, we can't take you back in the tanks. They ride on the rough side. We've radioed back for an ambulance. It will take awhile for that to get here. We were supposed to probe as far as this village up the road here—F-something-or-other," the captain said to Bill

"I believe it's called Feuchtwangen," Bill said.

The captain shrugs his shoulders. To him it's just another damn Nazi-infested village filled with fanatics, and they want to kill him. What the hell did he care what they called the place. He was supposed to go as far as F-something-or-other and pull back.

"We're supposed to start pulling back before sunset. We'll stay put until the ambulance arrives for you. Meantime, we're going to set up a defense here in case the SOBs come back this way," the captain said to Bill.

"While you're at it, there are a couple of things," Bill said. "There's a very young Dutch boy in the hospital up there and we need to save him. There's also a Doctor Meier up there and a whole bunch of German Lutheran nuns. Do what you can for them. They saved me. There's also a damn Nazi bastard up there—an older janitor. Shoot him."

U.S. infantrymen from the 12th Armored Division head up the hill toward the hospital.

When the ambulance arrives a young medic, a lieutenant, comes over to Bill.

"Jeez who got this guy drunk? He's wounded and now you've got him drunk!" the medic exclaims.

They load Bill in the ambulance and he is on his way back to the American lines.

"What's the date today?" Bill asks the medic. The time since he was shot down has been a blur. He has no idea how many days he evaded before the SS bastard shot him, or how long he was in the meadow left for dead, or how long he was in the hospital. He has been in-and-out of delirium so many times the entire experience seems a nightmare without end.

"I think it's April 21st," the medic said.

It seems a lot longer than two weeks since he was shot down. Several lifetimes have come-and-gone. He realizes his survival of the shoot-down of *Miss Steve* was a major miracle. He could so easily have been shot and killed by the Nazis at Ansbach. The schnauzer could have ripped him to shreds. Nazi soldiers by the bridge in the small village could have dusted him off the bicycle. An inch one way or the other and the shot drilled through him by the SS bastard could have finished him right there. The nightmare seems to have no end. But he has survived. He is still here.

Bill walks into the American field hospital just behind the front lines.

Battlefield casualties are streaming in, carted on jeeps, hauled in ambulances. Some are walking with hands, arms, heads wrapped in bandages.

Compared with the wounded he sees around him, Bill thinks he's in pretty good shape. You have to look carefully to see the hole through the right-hand pocket of his flight suit, and the exit hole in the back. The bloodstains have turned brown and could be mistaken for dirt.

A medic gives Bill a quick look and determines that while he has obviously been shot through the body, he does not appear to be in imminent danger of dying.

"On the surface it looks like you're in decent shape," the medic said. "We have no reason to keep you here. Do you think you can walk and sit on an airplane?" the medic asks. "If you can do that, we'll put you on a transport and send you to the hospital in Paris. Otherwise, we'll send you in an ambulance and that will be a six-to-eight hour rough ride, probably not the best thing for you right now."

"I can walk," Bill said. "I can walk."

The idea of an eight-hour ambulance ride over mostly dirt roads has no appeal to Bill. He still hurts like hell.

"Great. Now, I've got a problem and I need your help," the medic said. "We're a little understaffed up here and I have a bunch of Polish boys who are in bad shape. They've been German POWs since 1939. There's nothing we can do for them here and I need to get them out of our way and back to Paris. That transport is the only way I have right now of getting them out of here. You're going to be in charge of them. I want you to convince them to get on that plane and go to Paris. We are going to tell them you are a pilot and you have to reassure them it will be OK to get on that transport and fly to Paris."

"I don't speak Polish," Bill said

"We have a translator for you," the medic said.

At that the medic points toward the transport plane, gives Bill a smart salute and walks off.

Here is Bill. He has been shot through the body with his own .45. He has difficulty walking. He's now coming out of his alcoholic stupor from the brandy the tankers gave him. And he is put in charge of a dozen Polish ex-POWs.

Bill looks at the Poles and they are a sorry group. They are so emaciated their clothes hang on them like clothes on a scarecrow. Their cheeks are concave. Their eyes are bits of charcoal with no life in them. They are a beat-up bunch.

"I've been detailed to help you," a sergeant says walking up to Bill.

"Great. Do you speak Polish?" Bill asks.

"That's why they picked me. Halsted Street, Chicago," the sergeant said.

"Just north of North Avenue," Bill replies. "Do you have any chewing gum?"

"Tons of it," the sergeant said.

"Good, we're going to need it," Bill said.

The Poles start talking wildly to the sergeant. They wave their hands in the air as they all talk at once.

"They say if they get on that airplane the Germans will shoot them down and they'll die," the sergeant said.

"Tell them it is going to be a beautiful ride and the Luftwaffe is nowhere around," Bill said knowing full well that is a large fib. The damn Luftwaffe is still around last he knew.

There is more gesturing and intense talk from the Poles.

"They say they'll get sick on the airplane," the sergeant said. "They say they would rather walk to Paris."

"Give each of them a pack of chewing gum. Tell them nobody's going to get sick. Tell them I'm a fighter pilot, I know what I'm talking about. Tell them if they chew that gum on the airplane they will be just fine. No problems. Tell them it is going to be a beautiful ride," Bill said. "And tell them we are going to fly to Paris and tonight we will have a party and we are all going to get drunk as hell."

The sergeant translates. The Poles look at each other. Then they start to laugh. They board the transport. As the plane takes off the Poles are so excited they cheer.

En route to Paris Bill watches as the ex-POWs point and shout as they look out the airplane windows. Obviously, they have never been on an airplane. They are having a great time.

The transport is flying at fairly low altitude and is bouncing around.

Bill throws up. Even though he is sick he starts to laugh at himself. Here he is, smooth ace-pilot telling the Poles everything will be just fine…and who gets sick?

◆   ◆   ◆

Bill is admitted to the 250th General Hospital in Paris. American military doctors examine Bill and confirm, yes indeed he was shot through the right lower chest wall and there are no further procedures to be done. He is healing.

"How do I get a telegram off to my mother to let her know I'm OK?" Bill asks the doctor.

"I'll have someone see you about that," the doctor said.

◆   ◆   ◆

It takes two days for the Western Union telegram to reach the States. It arrives in Chicago at 11:21 p.m. on April 23.

There is a middle-of-the-night knock on the door at 1719 New England Avenue, Chicago. Bill's mother is shocked to see the Western Union delivery person at her door. Western Union telegrams are usually bad news. Her mind races as she thinks of her son Bill. She rips open the envelope.

"I AM SAFE… IN AMERICAN HANDS… SLIGHTLY WOUNDED … LETTER FOLLOWS … I MAY FOLLOW TOO … LOVE … BILL CULLERTON."

◆   ◆   ◆

Bill is moved to another wing of the 250th Hospital. This area—he decides—is designed to put some meat back on the bones of wounded Americans. The Government wants the boys to look good when they arrive back in the States.

The food is delicious. At the end of the corridor is a freezer filled with ice cream. There is also a malted milk-maker where Bill can make his own malt any time he wants. He can leave the hospital in the evening if he can walk. If he needs transportation someone always seems to have a jeep. And he goes to the bars with others from the hospital and they drink.

By the end of the third day, Bill confronts the medical supervisor on his wing.

"When do I get out of here?" Bill asks.

"You're in the 250th General Hospital. That means you are here for 30 days," the supervisor said.

"I'm not here for 30 days," Bill shakes his head.

"Oh yes you are," the supervisor replies.

After the supervisor leaves, Bill sees that another fellow is packing up, preparing to leave. He is a fellow named Rudy. Bill talked with Rudy a couple of days ago. He was an intelligence officer who allowed himself to be intentionally captured in North Africa so he could go inside the German POW camps and organize and assist the American POWs. Rudy told Bill he had to report to the 8th United States Army Air Force headquarters in England before returning to the States.

"I have a big favor to ask of you. I need to get out of this place. When you get to England, please call the 355th Fighter Group in Steeple Morden and talk with Father McHugh. Tell him the Americans are holding me prisoner in this hospital over here and I have to get back to Steeple Morden," Bill said.

"OK, I'll do it," Rudy said.

◆   ◆   ◆

At 11:00 p.m. on April 25, there is another knock on the door at 1719 New England Avenue in Chicago. There stands another Western Union delivery person. Again, Bill's mother rips open the envelope.

"THE SECRETARY OF WAR DESIRES ME TO EXPRESS HIS DEEP REGRET THAT YOUR SON 1 LT CULLERTON WILLIAM J HAS BEEN MISSING IN ACTION OVER GERMANY SINCE 08 APR 45...IF FURTHER DETAILS OR OTHER INFORMATION ARE RECEIVED YOU WILL BE PROMPTLY NOTIFIED PERIOD CONFIRMING LETTER FOLLOWS = J A ULIO THE ADJUTANT GENERAL."

Bill's mother rereads for the 100th time the first telegram she received two days ago. She looks at the date of the telegram from her son. April 23. However, the second telegram—dated April 25—leaves a lingering doubt. Why is she receiving a telegram reporting Bill missing when he has sent a telegram saying he is all right?

She knows her son. He probably has guessed there could be confusion as to his safety and wanted her to know directly from him that he is safe. She turns out the lights and goes back to bed.

◆   ◆   ◆

Bill is eating ice cream when the 250th General Hospital supervisor finds him.

"I don't know who you know, but you are out of here," the supervisor said.

"Hey, Rudy got through to Father McHugh!" Bill exclaims.

"He sure as hell did," the supervisor said. "You are supposed to be at Orly Field in one hour. We've got a jeep and we are sending you out there."

The jeep speeds Bill to Orly Field. He is driven out on the tarmac right up to a C-47. A sergeant salutes him and invites him to board.

Bill enters the passenger compartment. It is unlike any airplane he has ever seen. It looks like a living room.

Then Bill realizes he is the only passenger.

"I'm the only one going?" Bill asks the sergeant.

"Sir, this is General James Doolittle's private aircraft. You must have done something right," the sergeant said.

General James "Jimmy" Doolittle has sent his private aircraft to fly Bill Cullerton back to England. Bill is stunned. All he can imagine is that General Doolittle is repaying the 355th Fighter Group for the escort service they provided him. The General and a couple of top officers were checked out to fly P-51s. The General already had his air medal for the Pacific, awarded along with the Congressional Medal of Honor for flying bombers off the aircraft carrier to stun the Japanese early in the war. Now he—and the other two—wanted their European air medals. The 355th Fighter Group provided the escort service. Bill heard there were 60 Mustangs from the 355th accompanying General Doolittle and his party. This was General Doolittle's way of repaying the 355th.

"Would you like some tea? Biscuits?" the sergeant asks as the plane rolls for takeoff.

◆   ◆   ◆

The Western Union delivery person arrives—once again—at 1719 New England Avenue, Chicago on May 5 at 11:00 p.m. Even though Mrs. Ethel Cullerton has received two prior Western Union telegrams, her nerves are on edge. She rips open the envelope and reads:

"THE SECRETARY OF WAR DESIRES ME TO INFORM YOU THAT YOUR SON 1ST/LT CULLERTON WILLIAM J RETURNED TO MILITARY CONTROL REPORT FURTHER STATES HOSPI-TALIZED=J A ULIO THE ADJUTANT GENERAL."

◆   ◆   ◆

Bill is taken to the Wimpole Park Hospital near the Bassingbourn Airfield. He is not far from his base at Steeple Morden. Bill is very certain Father McHugh arranged all of this, including the flight on General Doolittle's private aircraft.

Bill is just dozing off when he hears a fellow coming down the aisle in the hospital ward.

"Here you go asshole," he said, then pitches something on the bed.

"Here you go asshole," he repeats, and again pitches something on the bed.

He arrives at Bill's bed. Bill looks at him.

"Hey, Joey Organ," Bill said. It was one of his classmates from Oak Park's Fenwick High School. Joey Organ was a small fellow, about five-foot-two-inches at most. He was all fight, but too small to play football so he was the Fenwick High School student manager.

"Cully. How the hell did you end up here?" Joey asks.

"So what are you passing out?" Bill asks.

"Oh, that's right. Here you go asshole," Joey said as he hands Bill his purple heart. They both laugh and decide as soon as Bill is able, they will go to one of the local pubs.

◆   ◆   ◆

The *Mums* visit the wounded Yanks every day to write letters for those who are too banged up to write, to bring special biscuits and other treats to those who can eat them, and generally to provide company and comfort.

For these British women it is a way to do their bit for *The War* effort. And their company is much appreciated by the Yanks.

Bill Cullerton is a good looking, 21-year-old who the *Mums* could tell had been through an ordeal of some sort. It isn't apparent as he lies in the hospital bed exactly what is wrong with him. The *Mums* are too polite to ask direct questions. However, they take it upon themselves to bring special treats to the Yanks they think are looking thin and physically drained. Bill, one of the *Mums* decides, is in need of some special treats.

◆   ◆   ◆

From his hospital bed in Wimpole Park on May 12, 1945, Bill writes to his folks in flawless penmanship:

"Dear Mom & Dad:

"I received one of your letters today, the one written while Dad was filling out Goats gas application.

"First of all I'll describe my wound for you, 'security' permits it now. I was shot with a pistol, the bullet entered my right lower chest wall and came out near the middle of my back. It pierced the liver and kidney but thanks to the grace of God, I'm OK. The finest doctors over here have examined me and they can't find a thing wrong. So you have no need whatsoever to worry about me. I feel better now than I ever did. The only reason I'm telling you about the wound is because of that phone call. Just think, a June wedding.

"I can't think of anything more except that I sure do love and miss my family. Bill."

Bill's parents have alerted *the groom* that they have heard from *the bride* and the wedding date has been set!

◆   ◆   ◆

Father McHugh and Dr. Earl Walker appear at Bill's bedside. Dr. Walker gives him a quick look and concludes he is healing very well.

"You are a lucky fellow," Dr. Walker tells Bill. "To survive having a .45 slug go through your body like that is a major miracle. That gun barrel must have been right up against you when it was fired."

"That's exactly right," Bill said.

"If that pistol had been back about a foot away from your body, there would have been a hole in your back the size of a grapefruit and that would have been that," Dr. Walker said. "I think we should get you out of here and on your way back to the States," Dr. Walker said.

Bill leaves the hospital with Father McHugh and Dr. Walker, on his way back to the Steeple Morden Airfield, and on his way home—back to Chicago.

Bill flies from Scotland to New York. Then it's a train ride to Washington, D.C., for intelligence debriefing and then another train ride to Chicago. He arrives at Union Station in Chicago June 12, 1945—two days before his father's birthday, and 18 days before a major ceremony.

◆   ◆   ◆

On Saturday June 30, 1945 crowds gather outside Ascension Church in Oak Park. A real *War Hero* is to be married. Hundreds of relatives and friends fill every pew in the church. Those outside just want to catch a glimpse of the couple.

All the Chicago newspapers carry the wedding story with photographs and headlines such as: "Ace takes a bride."

When asked how he feels about the wedding, one of the Chicago newspapers reports *the groom* is extremely nervous and quotes him: "I'm more scared of a big wedding than I am of all the flak over Europe." The newspaper went on to say Bill "completed his matrimonial mission today without a mishap."

And the newspaper has this to say about *the bride:* "Blond Mrs. Cullerton, beautiful in white satin, with yards of veil, appeared unafraid."

PART V

For The Ages

19

Fixer & Dedication

St. Catherine's Church—May 1993

Fifty veterans of the 355th Fighter Group are scheduled to arrive in England May 12, 1993, for the celebration marking the 50th anniversary of the Group's arrival at the Steeple Morden Airfield.

The Friends of St. Catherine's Church in Litlington arrange for a master stonemason to begin work April 19 to remove the old glass, repair the masonry and make all preparations for installation of the window honoring the 355th Fighter Group. The master stonemason estimates the work will take one week to complete. The window dedication is scheduled to take place Sunday, May 16.

Certainly a full month should be more than enough for the master stonemason to complete his work, and for the fixer to install the new window.

Great care must be taken when working on this ancient monument. Bits of stone have crumbled, especially in the uppermost reaches of the tracery with all of its intricate masonry carvings. There has been settling through the ages. Windowsills run a little off kilter. Stone pillars separating the lights may appear to the eye to be in the perpendicular, however they may be out-of-plumb by as much as four or five inches over their eight-foot height.

Wherever iron bars have been attached to the ancient stone to hold old windows in place, there is potential for decay—trouble not found until the iron is removed. Iron corrodes and eats away deep in the stone leaving unsightly brackish yellow stains.

The master stonemason chips away at the damage of the ages, places new pieces in the tracery, and patches delicately where necessary. The work goes on for the first full week…and continues into the second week.

It begins to appear to the Friends of St. Catherine's that the master stonemason might still be at work when the 355th reunion attendees arrive.

The window remains in the shipping crate on the St. Catherine's Church floor, just as it arrived from the States on Good Friday.

Warden of St. Catherine's Church Pamela Sharp and the other church leaders in Litlington become more concerned as the *Yanks* arrival for their 50th reunion and the dedication of the window is now within a week. If the *fixer*—the chap who actually installs the window—encounters any difficulties there could be real trouble.

Finally the master stonemason completes his work.

On Monday, May 10, Dean Cullum of Cambridge Stained Glass arrives to install the window. In the ancient tradition of stained glass work, Dean Cullum is the *fixer*—the person who takes the panels of stained glass and cements them in place.

It is with trepidation Dean Cullum removes the first section measuring two feet wide, by three feet high from the packing crate. The first thing he notices is there is very little painting. Instead, the work is hundreds of pieces of glass fit together to make the images. He holds the panel up to the light. The colors are vivid. This is strikingly different from any work he has seen before.

Here is stained glass work produced in the States by a *Yank* to be placed in a 600-year-old church window opening that has just been rehabilitated by an English master stonemason. The odds seem very remote that any stained glass work will fit in place under such conditions. No matter, he must proceed.

Using the scaffolding left by the master stonemason, Dean Cullum carries the first section up the scaffolding. This section—with the 8th United States Army Air Force emblem in dark blue with vivid yellow wings and a red star center—should slide up through the intricate masonry of the center window opening. He positions the panel just below the tracery, moves the left side of the section into the channel in the stone window well, then positions the right side and slides the panel back ever so gently. Then he pushes the entire section up through the tracery. It moves up and into place without resistance. It is a perfect fit. Dean Cullum cements the section in place.

Dean Cullum is quite amazed. This might go together after all!

He returns to the crate for the panel that should slide directly under the uppermost section. Here is the 355th coat-of-arms and the motto: *Our Might Always.* He repeats the gentle fitting and this piece also goes in perfectly.

Dean Cullum goes back to the crate for the bottom section. It has the hand painted, fired lettering: *355th Fighter Group—July 1943–July 1945.* It is too much to hope that this will also go in place as easily as the first two. If it is an inch too long, it will not fit. He holds his breath and repeats the motions of inserting the section. It fits exactly as it should.

Within four hours of arriving at St. Catherine's Church, Dean Cullum completes fitting all nine sections of the 355th memorial window in place.

Metal bars are cemented in and the window sections are secured to the bars to provide extra strength to prevent bowing and settling through the ages.

The window is installed and the Friends of St. Catherine's—and Dean Cullum—breathe an enormous sigh of relief.

◆　　　◆　　　◆

Fifty veterans of the 355th Fighter Group walk from their motor coach up the stone walkway to the entrance to St. Catherine's Church. It is Thursday, May 13. They are going to have a preview look at *The Window at St. Catherine's.* There will be more time this day for a good look at the window than there will be at the dedication services this coming Sunday.

Church Warden Pamela Sharp is standing in the altar area near the newly installed window and she watches the veterans as they approach the window made in their honor.

Bill Cullerton is among the first to view the window.

Pamela Sharp watches as one by one they come around and see sunlight illuminating the stained glass to a full brilliance of blues, yellows and reds. They see the great American eagle, its wings spread over the blazing red and yellow emblem of the 355th with the glistening dagger streaking through the center. There are the silhouettes of the airplanes they maintained and flew from the airfield not more than a quarter-mile away—the P-47 Thunderbolt and the P-51 Mustang. At the top of the center window, brilliantly illuminated in the full sun, is the 8th United States Army Air Force emblem, the very emblem they all wore during *The War.*

Pamela watches as the tears begin to flow as one after the other these now older warriors wipe their eyes. *The Window at St. Catherine's* touches their souls.

◆   ◆   ◆

The Bishop of Ely sends his regrets at not being able to attend the dedication of *The Window at St. Catherine's* on Sunday, May 16, 1993.

The maker of the window also sends his regrets.

However, there is some discussion that the motives behind the two "regrets" might be quite different.

In the latter case we know we wanted Bill Cullerton and the other 49 veterans attending the service of dedication to take the full salute. The window was made to honor them.

The Bishop of Ely designated in his place the Bishop of Huntingdon The Right Reverend Gordon Roe. It was most appropriate that the Bishop from Cambridge would be so designated.

St. Catherine's Church is full and overflowing with 350 folks inside the church. There are so many who wish to attend the dedication service, tickets are issued for seats. For a small village, this is an event the likes of which no one can recall.

An honor guard of the North Hertfordshire Royal Air Force Cadets lines the walkway to the Church entrance.

Trumpeters from the Band of the Royal Air Force Regiment open the ceremonies with a fanfare that rings through St. Catherine's Church.

There is a prayer and then the singing the National Anthem of the United States of America.

The Chapel Choir of Clare College, Cambridge performs.

Pamela Sharp and David Crow read the first and second lessons.

And the Bishop of Huntingdon—with Bill and Steve Cullerton, Church Wardens Pamela Sharp and John Jenner at his side—dedicates *The Window at St. Catherine's*.

While this was the official dedication, another memorable ceremony would be held in St. Catherine's Church 12 years later.

20

Victory-Europe+60 Years

Litlington & Steeple Morden—May 2005

Only three of the 355th Fighter Group veterans make it back to England in May of 2005 for the Victory-Europe Plus 60-Years celebration held in their honor and in honor of the British veterans of World War Two.

St. Catherine's Church in Litlington is—once again—filled to overflowing on Sunday, May 8. This is exactly 60 years to-the-day of the German surrender to the Allies in World War Two.

The British Broadcasting Company sends a camera to cover the event.

Secretary of the 355th Fighter Group veterans organization Bob Kuhnert, Flight Crew Chief Julius Moseley, and Bill Cullerton are seated in the front pews at St. Catherine's this Sunday morning.

Bill Cullerton has with him two, 15-year-old grandsons.

Following addresses, ministries of the church leaders, hymns, the singing of the British and American National Anthems, there is a final talk given by Bill Cullerton.

Bill climbs the circular steps to mount the 10-foot high pulpit, which dates from the 15th century.

Looking at his old comrade Crew Chief Julius Moseley, Bill starts:

"Julius, I could have taken a P-51 to ten-thousand feet faster than I climbed up here."

Three-hundred-and-fifty of us laugh.

"In 1943 the Three-Five-Five Fighter Group of the Eighth Army Air Force moved into these environs. We were a rather large assortment of bold...rather loud...rather precocious...very lonesome and lost young men. We flooded the countryside, and a blending of two cultures began.

And you know it didn't take long and our English friends soon opened hearth and heart to these odd Yanks. Tea and cookies—or crumpets as we called them—were served it seems 24 hours a day, right across the road here. There were certainly free dart lessons at any pub for any Yank who would dare to challenge the local dart champion...and there might be a pint or two bet on the side.

"And the tower at St. Catherine's...I can't describe the feeling of total relief when you would break out of the solid overcast and have the tower say: 'Can you see the church tower? Can *you* see the church tower?' That was our home. When we saw the tower...we were home...we had made it. God it meant so much to us...it means so much to us.

"Our affection and respect for our English friends is going to last long after all of us are dust.

"I don't want to personalize this, but I want to tell you that 60 years ago today I was in a hospital not far from here after having been brought back from Germany. The recovery was absolutely spectacular.

"I don't know how many *Mums* visited us, but we had a hundred *Mums*. And they fawned over us. They helped us write letters home.

"I had a very special *Mum*.

"She said to me: 'You know what Yank, you need a little of my cherry cobbler.'

"I said: 'I do...I'm sure I do.'

"She baked it. She brought it. And I consumed it.

"I can picture her and I don't know who she was. But if she were here today...I would walk down...I would kneel down in front of her...and take her hands in mine...and I would caress them.

"Speaking for the two-thousand Yanks of the Three-Five-Five, I have to tell you that we love you guys.

"God bless you. God bless us all."

And among the 350 of us in St. Catherine's Church this morning, there is not a dry eye.

◆   ◆   ◆

Bright sunshine illuminates *The Window at St. Catherine's* as Bill Cullerton and I gaze upon it. There it is for the ages.

Appendix A

About Bill Cullerton

Following World War Two, Bill Cullerton never piloted an airplane again. He and his wife Steve have five children, 19 grandchildren, and three great-children. Bill is chairman of the board "emeritus" of the Cullerton Company, a manufacturer's representative firm in the fishing and outdoor business. For two decades he hosted *The Great Outdoors Show* on Chicago's WGN-Radio. Bill served on dozens of boards-of-directors in the fishing and outdoor trade. He is an honorary trustee of Chicago's John G. Shedd Aquarium. For his work in conservation and as an advocate for outdoorsmen and outdoor issues, in 2000 the State of Illinois honored Bill by naming the 4,000-acre Illinois Beach State Park along with North Point Marina the *Cullerton Complex*. Bill was the youngest member ever inducted into the International Sport Fishing Hall of Fame, and is listed in the book, *America's 100 Sportfishing Legends.* He is a member of the board of the McGraw Wildlife Federation. He is in the Illinois Military Aviation Hall of Fame and is enshrined in the Champlin Fighter Aces Museum in Mesa, Arizona.

Bill Cullerton's Citations

Distinguished Service Cross
Silver Star
Distinguished Flying Cross with Three Clusters
Purple Heart
Air Medal with Seven Clusters
Presidential Unit Citation

Prisoner of War Medal
European-African-Middle Eastern Campaign Medal
World War II Victory Medal
Polish Medal: Warsaw Uprising Cross
Russian Medal: Order of The Great Patriotic War
French Medal: Croix de Guerre

APPENDIX B

Acknowledgments

Special thanks in preparation of this book to Bill and Steve Cullerton; Bob Kuhnert, Secretary-Treasurer 355th Fighter Group Veterans Association; David Crow, Chairman of the 355th Fighter Group Committee in the UK, and Lorinda Drake Crow[1]; Pamela Sharp, former Church Warden, St. Catherine's Church, Litlington, and David Sharp; William A. Rooney, Secretary of the 40th Bombardment Group, co-author *The Enola Gay and the Smithsonian Institution;* Bill Marshall, author *Angels, Bulldogs & Dragons, The 355th Fighter Group in World War II;* Barbara L. Dobbertin, movie recordings.

Additional Acknowledgments

Cynthia Clayton, OBE
The late Jim Clayton
Peter D. Griffiths
Jill Jarman
Jean Jarman
Maureen Huffer
Pat Leach
Kath Lunness
John Jenner, St. Catherine's Church Warden
Pamela Sharp, Former St. Catherine's Church Warden

---

1. *Lorinda's late father served in the 355th FG during WWII and took his British bride back to the U.S. from London.*

355th Fighter Group
United Kingdom Committee

David Crow, Chairman
Kenneth J. Jarman
Peter G. Jarman
Brian A. Huffer
John H. Lunness
Raymond E. Leach, Sdn Ldr, MBE, RAF Retired
Graham Jarman
David A. Sharp

APPENDIX C
Bibliography

Most material for this work was gathered from the author's extensive personal notes, correspondence, records, and on-location interviews, recordings and observations. Bill Marshall's book *Angels, Bulldogs & Dragons; The 355th Fighter Group in World War II* was of exceptional value in preparation of this book. Other books cited below were used almost exclusively to confirm data.

Bradley, Omar N. *A General's Life*. New York: Simon & Schuster, 1974

Eisenhower, David. *Eisenhower at War 1943–45*. New York: Random House, Inc., 1986

Foss, Joe & Brennan, Matthew. *Top Guns*. New York: Pocket Books, 1991

Freeman, Roger A. *Mustang at War*. Garden City, New York: Doubleday and Company, Inc., 1974

Marshall, Bill. *Angels, Bulldogs & Dragons; The 355th Fighter Group in World War II*. Mesa, Arizona: Champlin Fighter Museum, 1984

Wells, Ken. *Steeple Morden Strafers*. Baldock, Herts. United Kingdom: Egon Publishers, Ltd.,1994

APPENDIX D

About the Author

John Dobbertin, Jr. is a 1964 graduate of the University of Michigan. He completed a two-year University of Michigan journalism fellowship as subeditor of *The Daily-Star,* Beirut, Lebanon. In Beirut he also taught English-as-a-second-language at Hagazian College. He wrote feature stories in Asia Minor and Western Europe for Copley News Agency. He was a reporter and feature writer for the *Kalamazoo Gazette,* Kalamazoo, Michigan. He joined the public relations staffs of Johnson Motors then Zenith Radio Corporation. He directed the Chicago Boat Show and a large trade event for the pleasure boating industry before co-founding a public event and trade show production company. He and his partner sold the company to Capital Cities-American Broadcasting Companies, which in turn became part of Walt Disney Enterprises.

APPENDIX E

Who Saved Bill Cullerton

In interviews in 1992 and 1993 Bill Cullerton was fairly certain he was res-cued near Feuchtwangen, Germany, in mid-April 1945 by a spearhead of the 14th Armored Division. Bill was certain it was a very big black gunner on a tank who pointed a machine gun at him and shouted: "Don't move."

When the author reviewed the movement of the 14th AD in mid-April, 1945 it was apparent they were in the vicinity of Nurnberg, to the north-east of Feuchtwangen. This seemed to match Bill's memory of events. The first two editions of this book have the 14th AD spearhead as the combat unit that rescued Bill Cullerton.

Prior to publishing the author posted on the Internet site of the 14th AD his interest in contacting any veteran who might recall rescuing an American pilot near Feuchtwangen, Germany. That led to contact with the 14th AD Veterans Association, including an invitation to address a reunion of the group in LaCrosse, Wisconsin. It was during this reunion the author began to realize the story of the rescue by the 14th AD was not adding up.

If the 14th Armored Division did not rescue Bill Cullerton, who did? Research and help from World War Two veterans and historians brought the answer.

In early January 1945 the 12th Armored Division was assigned to stop the German advance at the Gambsheim-Herrlisheim bridgehead on the Rhine River. In this engagement the 12th AD suffered large losses requir-ing 1,700 replacements (*Speed Is the Password: The Story of the 12th Armored Division,* published by the *Stars & Stripes* in Paris in 1944-45). This was at the same time as *The Battle of the Bulge* in which the United States armed forces suffered significant infantry losses. Manpower—especially infantrymen—was in short supply. To make up the shortages, the 12th AD received three companies—12 platoons—of black infantrymen (*The United States Army in World War Two, Special Studies: The Employment of Negro Troops* by Ulysses Lee, 1966).

The United States armed forces in World War Two were racially segregated. There were exceptions, and the 12th AD was one of those exceptions. The attachment of blacks to armored divisions was a watershed moment in American military history. Ulysses Lee's book goes into great detail on how this came to be. Lee notes: "The plan itself represented a major break with traditional Army policy, for it proposed mixing Negro soldiers into otherwise white units neither on a quota nor a smaller unit basis but as individuals fitted in where needed." Lee also notes of the three companies attached to the 12th AD: "All of these companies were used as armored infantry in support of tanks or with tank support....The companies attacked dismounted or mounted on tanks...."

In the *Hellcat News* of April 2006, the 12th AD Historian Edward Waszak wrote: "On April 19 (1945), the 12th Armored Division is in the area of Feuchtwangen. Combat Command A is in Schwabach. Combat Command B and Combat Command R are in Ansbach. All three Combat Commands head for Feuchtwangen to launch a two-prong attack on a south axis toward the Danube River. It appears that all three Commands passed through Feuchtwangen on April 20/21 and my guess is that the first scouting group probably was from CCR according to information in the *Seventh U.S. Army—Report of Operations,* page 805, and *Journal of Operations of the 17th Armored Infantry Battalion,* pages 11/12."

Deputy National Historian of the 14th AD Jim Lankford notes in correspondence with the author: "....there were Black troops serving as armored infantry with the 12th Armored Division, and elements of the 12th AD did operate in the immediate area of Feuchtwangen. At that point in the war it was common practice for infantrymen to ride on the backs of the advancing tanks. One of the infantrymen would usually man the tank's .50 cal. while the tank commander stayed in the turret, and paid attention to his tank. My guess is that Bill Cullerton was liberated by a tank of the 12th AD, and he saw one of the Black armored infantrymen on the .50 cal., not one of the tankers. So his memory is probably 100% correct. I'll bet he just mistook the Black infantryman on the .50 cal. as a member of the tank crew."

The 17th Armored Infantry Battalion was a unit of the 12th AD and in their *Historical Information—Plunge into Bavaria,* author F. George Hatt, Jr., writes:

"On Saturday, 14 April 1945, the 17th Armored Infantry Battalion launched its southward thrust following the *Romanesque Road,* a pathway which had been used by the Romans in the first to fifth centuries while they dominated Europe. Though the 17th Armored Infantry Battalion's spearhead movement was rapid, dangerous episodes presented themselves daily. Again snipers, mortars, panzerfausts, artillery, and antitank mines were hindrances along the way. On the other hand, citizens in the more ancient towns such as those which had survived since the Middle Ages, wanted to surrender without a fight so that the venerable houses and public buildings would be preserved. For example: Dinkelsbuhl, Feuchtwangen, and Rothenburg…."

In May 2006, 12th AD Historian Ed Waszak wrote to the author:

"I found several sources that put the 12th Armored Division in Feuchtwangen on April 19/20, 1945. I could find no other units there at that time. Using Bill's story of the rescue, the first American units following the Germans were the spearhead units of the 12th AD. That was Combat Command R, led by the 17th Armored Infantry Battalion and the 23rd Tank Battalion. The task force was moving rapidly from town-to-town, bypassing surrendering Germans, liberating Allied prisoner of war camps, concentration camps and eliminating resistance…."

One of the officers of the 12th Armored Division Veterans Association, John E. Critzas (gunner, A Co. 714th Tank Battalion), told the author in a telephone conversation it would be his best estimate that the units that rescued Bill Cullerton were the 23rd Tank Battalion and the 17th Armored Infantry Battalion of the 12th Armored Division.

"The tanks—accompanied by infantry—always led the spearheads," Critzas said.

978-0-595-36921-
0-595-36921-9

Made in the USA
Lexington, KY
01 October 2010